Kites: An Historical Survey

KITES
An Historical Survey

CLIVE HART

Revised and Expanded Second Edition

PAUL P. APPEL, *Publisher*
Mount Vernon, New York

Library of Congress Cataloging in Publication Data

Hart, Clive.
    Kites, an historical survey.

    Bibliography: p.
    Includes index.
    1. Kites—History.   I. Title.
TL759.3.H3 1981   629.133'32'09   81-1252
ISBN 0-911858-40-7 (Clothbound)   AACR2
ISBN 0-911858-38-5 (Paperbound)

Dust jacket illustration courtesy *Kite Lines*, the
quarterly journal of the worldwide kite community:

Jalbert Parafoil being flown by G. William Tyrrell, Jr.,
at Ocean City, Maryland in 1978. Photography by
Theodore L. Manekin.

FOR HELEN

He feels the pressure of the blast as if he himself must stand against it, and with his whole being he participates in the flight. He walks on the earth, but a part of him seems to struggle with the elements and rise to the clouds. With the little shining sail he moves through space and hurries across the firmament. When the sun shines on its white surface it is as if he himself were bathed in light. Inertia is momentarily overcome, and the heavy earthling is made one with the nimble winds.

— YRJÖ HIRN

Acknowledgments

My thanks are due most particularly to Mr Charles H. Gibbs-Smith, who not only read the typescript and wrote the Foreword, but was inexhaustibly generous with his time, ideas, and learning. I owe to him some of the best material in the book.

Mr F. H. Smith, Librarian of the Royal Aeronautical Society, gave me further friendly and highly effective assistance with references.

For scholarly help and encouragement, and for the granting of copyright permission, I should like to thank the following individuals and institutions: Badische Landesbibliothek; Surendra Bahadur, of *Go Fly a Kite*, New York; George J. Becker, Jr., of the Ryan Aeronautical Company; the Superintendent of the A. G. Bell Museum; the staff of the British Museum Reading Room; the British Council Representatives in Bangkok and Tokyo; Robert V. Bruce; Dr Edwin H. Bryan, of the Bernice P. Bishop Museum, Honolulu; the staff of the Department of Ethnography of the British Museum; the Department of Tourism, Malaysia; the Dominion Museum, Wellington; John Fairfax and Sons, Ltd.; the Field Museum of Natural History, Chicago; Robert H. Fowler, of *Civil War Times*; Stadt- und Universitätsbibliothek, Frankfurt am Main; Gale and Polden, Ltd.; Robert E. Hart, Australia's only professional kite-flier (not related to the author); Thor Heyerdahl; the Director of Information Services, Kuala Lumpur; Morley Kennerley; Francis A. Lord; Dr Eric Marson; Colin Mayrhofer; John Morwood; the Director of the Museum of Applied Arts and Sciences, Ultimo, N.S.W.; the National Geographic Society; the Director of the National Library of Ireland; Dr Joseph Needham; Niedersächsische Staats- und Universitätsbibliothek, Göttingen; the editors of *Notes and Queries*, and the Oxford University Press; Österreichische Nationalbibliothek; the staff of the Reading Room of the Public Library of N.S.W.; Radio Times Hulton Picture Library; Miss Elizabeth Ralph, City Archivist of the Bristol Archives Office; Francis Rogallo; Routledge and Kegan Paul, Ltd.; the Royal Aeronautical Society;

the Librarian of the Royal Society; the Royal Society of New South Wales; the director of the Science Museum, South Kensington; the editors of *Scientific American*; W. H. Shaw, of Qantas; Professor Godfrey Tanner; Marie and Ric Tietze; the Charles E. Tuttle Company; the United States Weather Bureau; the Vanguard Press, Inc.; Daniel S. Wentz II, of NASA; Yale University Press; West Australian Newspapers, Ltd.; Will Yolen, President of the International Kitefliers Association; Württembergische Landesbibliothek; Frank Zabrana.

My thanks are due also for the practical assistance of my friends and family – especially to my wife, for her love of the subject and for her criticism of my early drafts; to Robin Smith, for photographic and other assistance; to Julian Croft, for his valuable co-volatilism; and to Joan Budgen, who flew kites on Primrose Hill.

Finally, I must give thanks to the memory of my father, who made my first kite and, like the Thai mandarins, let it fly all night.

Contents

Plates

Between pages 32 and 33

Between pages 96 and 97

Foreword

by Charles H. Gibbs-Smith

It may seem curious that until now there has never appeared an authoritative history of the kite. But kites have seldom been treated seriously as a branch of aviation (which they are), nor has their absorbing story often been appreciated by historians, let alone by the general public. If one mentions the word 'kite' to the average man or woman, it can only conjure up images of sweating little boys tugging desperately on their kite-strings in order to coax these wayward offspring into the air; or of blasé individuals of all ages holding their strings in a would-be nonchalant manner, occasionally glancing aloft to check that their charges are riding safely among the birds – at times a pull on the string is the only assurance that the 'thing' is still up there, in or above the clouds. The kite-flyer of today is all too often completely ignorant of another pull of the fascinating history that he has there in his hand.

The kite, in its humbler function, can boast a longer consecutive service to humanity as a plaything than any other, except the doll; and it will clearly continue in that role until the end of time. But as the variety of its uses comes under historical scrutiny we find kites being employed for military signalling, and – fitted with flutes – for frightening the life out of superstitious enemies cowering in their tents; as aids to oriental fishermen, when their hooks are suspended from above and no tell-tale shadows are thrown upon the water; as transports for airborne firework displays; as probers of clouds for the secrets of lightning; as aerial tugs to haul horse-less carriages across land, and boats across water; as flying observation posts for the soldier in battle; and as savers of life in the last war when they raised the radio aerials from the life-rafts of aircrews adrift at sea.

As an aeronautical historian, the kite is, of course, sacred to me; for it was the prototype of the aeroplane-wing, and may be regarded as a tethered glider. With the passive windmill made active, and the captive kite made free, the idea of the powered aeroplane could take wings and fly.

So, at last, it has been Clive Hart who has written the history we have been without, for so long: it is not only the first proper history of this type of aircraft, it is a classic in its own right, and has been eminently worth waiting for over the years. The author is not only an expert in the history of the subject; he is also a practical kite-man among the kiters, who can coax his craft off the ground, and send it up to ride the winds, along with the best of them. But that is not all. Clive Hart comes to technological history from the arts, and he can write – with style.

Preface to the Revised Edition

Since this book was written, nearly fifteen years ago, there has been a rapid growth of interest in kites. Not only have kite-flying clubs flourished in many countries, but professional aerodynamicists have become more seriously concerned than ever before in practical applications of the kite principle. Many new books have been published dealing with virtually every branch of the subject and several kiting journals have been founded.

The first edition of *Kites: an Historical Survey* has been out of print for a number of years. When contemplating the preparation of a revised edition, I necessarily gave serious thought to the new place which it would hold in the literature. Rather than attempt to duplicate the excellent work which has recently appeared on eastern kites, modern kites, and new technological developments, I thought it best to continue to concentrate on the area with which the book was always most concerned, namely the very early history of the subject. Accordingly I have made only a few changes in the chapters on exotic and modern kites. Elsewhere the changes range from the correction of occasional typos and small factual errors to the complete rewriting of Chapter 4, 'Early European Kites.' Many new plates and figures have been introduced, and I have appended to the original bibliography a check-list of additional material mainly relevant to the prehistory of kites.

C.H.

University of Essex, Colchester
May 1980

Introduction

During the two and a half thousand years of its existence the kite has proved itself a most remarkably versatile technological invention. It has been used for carrying men, for fishing, for towing anything from torpedoes to carriages, for providing gunnery targets, for signalling, for raising telephone wires and radio antennae, for aerial photography; and of course at the turn of the century it was an indispensable part of the meteorologist's equipment.

A really thorough study of the kite would need an historian expert in a dauntingly large number of fields. He would have to be skilled, for example, in aeronautics, anthropology, mythology, and meteorology; he would need to have travelled extensively in the east and throughout Oceania; and he would benefit from a working knowledge of several languages, including Japanese, Mandarin, and Polynesian. I cannot claim to have any special training in any of these fields (though reading and learning about kites has proved very educational). I have therefore had to rely heavily on secondary sources for much of what does not concern the practical making and flying of kites. (The most important of the sources are indicated by an asterisk in the bibliography.) This book is not, therefore, specially orientated towards any of the above fields. It is, rather, a general introduction to the subject in all its forms.

What is a kite? Is a balloon with wings to be considered a kite? If an entirely non-rigid parachute is made to support itself on the end of a string, will this satisfy the definition? The boundary between kites on the one hand, and balloons, gliders, parachutes, etc., on the other, is not a sharp one. I think a kite may nevertheless be usefully defined as a heavier-than-air machine held to the earth by means of a flexible line and capable of rising to a positive angle with the horizon as the result of forces created by wind-pressure. The definition does not, therefore, include kite-balloons, which function to some extent as kites, but are lighter than air. It does, however, include totally non-rigid aerodynes, such as the parachute mentioned above.

The most elegant and beautiful kites, together with the greatest ingenuity in their practical application, are to be found in the east. My first three chapters provide a survey of oriental kites, but the bulk of this book is devoted to the development of the technologically more important, if less attractive, western kites.

The variety of possible shapes is virtually endless. In most western countries, with the exception of the U.S.A., the number of designs with which children are familiar is very limited, including only a few bow and plane-surface kites, with perhaps one or two box kites. Even in the U.S., familiarity with a really large selection of kites is by no means common. Since the invention and widespread use of the aeroplane, adult interest in the kite has almost vanished. Its relegation, in most western minds, to the status of a toy, has meant the virtual oblivion of some of the most beautiful and ingenious designs. I hope that this book may help to remind readers of the advanced state of development which kites once attained.

C.H.

University of Newcastle, N.S.W.
May 1967

1 | Origins; China

The place of origin of the kite is fairly certain: China. It was known there some centuries before Christ and soon spread throughout south-east Asia and the Pacific generally. But who flew the first kite, and what sort of kite it would have been, are questions to which we can give only the most tentative answers. Theories have abounded: Needham mentions Waley's interesting but unlikely suggestion that the kite was 'derived from an ancient Chinese method of shooting off an arrow with a line attached to it, so that both arrow and prey could be recovered by hauling it in';[1] some have supposed that it might rather have been derived from another object on the end of a string–the bull-roarer;[2] and Needham himself offers the amusing but far from facetious suggestion that the first kite might have been a Chinese farmer's hat held by a string. My own speculations on this matter have centred on the similarity of the kite to the pennon or banner, and on the custom in many places of allowing banners to stream out in the wind either from a cord or from a flexible rod. In past centuries the personal banner was common among eastern dignitaries, while in fifteenth and sixteenth century Europe[3] the distinction between it and the kite was still somewhat blurred. It would seem quite natural to make a banner more clearly visible by stiffening it with light rods placed across it. Once this has been done the kite has virtually been invented.

[1] Needham, J., *Science and Civilisation in China*, Vol. 4, Pt. 2, Cambridge, 1965, p. 576. Needham's chapters constitute the definitive study in English of the history of the kite in China.

[2] *Ibid.*, p. 577.

[3] See Plischke, H., 'Alter und Herkunft des Europäischen Flächendrachens.' *Nachrichten von der Gesellschaft der Wissenschaften zu Göttingen*, Phil.-Hist. Kl, N.F., Fachgr. 2, Vol. 2, No. 1, 1936, pp. 5–6.

However it originated, the kite rapidly acquired religious, magical, and ceremonial significance in many of those parts of the world to which it spread. In at
least some civilizations, including the Polynesian, kites seem to have had some
function as symbols of an external soul. They were closely associated with deities and
heroes, and were a means of contact with heavenly regions. Professor Haddon, in his
well known book *The Study of Man*, stresses the idea of the kite as an external soul
and, developing the concept in a very attractive passage, suggests a possible physical
origin:

> If we grant, and there is to my mind very good reason for so doing, that the kite
> was a religious symbol of the primitive Indonesian race, we may fairly go one
> step further and suggest that the kite itself is merely the liberated soul of a canoe.
> Amongst a seafaring folk this accident must often arise, and the excitement of
> hauling down a sail that had blown away might very well lead to the process
> being intentionally repeated on a small scale.
>   It is tempting to imagine that as the sails of a canoe are virtually the life of a
> canoe–that is, the source of its movement, the loss of which leaves behind it an
> inert log at the mercy of the elements, so the kite by analogy may have come to be
> regarded as the 'external soul' or 'life-token' of the owner.[1]

Because of the uncertain boundary between kites and other flying machines, it
is not easy to decide what may be the earliest references to kites in China. Kites made
of wood or cloth may have existed there over two thousand years ago, but the term
'paper kite' which is sometimes used of them in the literature is anachronistic, since
rag-paper was not invented until A.D. 105.[2]

There is a well known story (recorded in a number of variants) concerning the
invention of a wooden dove. The artisan concerned is either Mo Ti or Kungshu
Phan, both contemporaries of Confucius. A typical version is translated by
Needham:

> Mo Tzu made a wooden kite . . . which took three years to complete. It could
> indeed fly, but after one day's trial it was wrecked. His disciples said 'What skill
> the Master has to be able to make a wooden kite fly!' But he answered 'It is not
> as clever as making a wooden ox-yoke peg . . . They only use a short piece of
> wood, eight-tenths of a foot in length, costing less than a day's labour, yet it can
> pull 30 *tan*, travelling far, taking great strain, and lasting many years. Yet I have

[1] Haddon, A. C., *The Study of Man*, London, 1898, pp. 251–2.
[2] Laufer, B., *The Prehistory of Aviation*, Chicago, 1928, p. 35.

worked three years to make this kite which has been ruined after one day's use.' Hui Tzu heard of it and said: 'Mo Tzu is indeed ingenious, but perhaps he knows more about making yoke-pegs than about making wooden kites.'[1]

In another version of the story, the bird stayed aloft for three days without coming down, while in a third it is said that Kungshu Phan also devised wooden man-lifting kites which were flown over a city in a state of siege.

In both Chinese and western literature doubt has of course been expressed about the accuracy of these reports, and in any case it is by no means clear that Mo Ti's dove is to be considered a kite as we understand the word now. Laufer, in his excellent study of the prehistory of aviation,[2] is fairly sure that it was not, but Needham is inclined to think that it might indeed have been a kite. There, in a state of doubt, the matter will probably have to remain.

The earliest date unambiguously ascribed to the kite in China is *ca.* 200 B.C. This is found in a story which is probably the most widespread account of the kite's origin. General Han Hsin (*d.* 196 B.C.) is said to have flown a kite over a palace in order to judge the distance between his army and the palace walls, so that a tunnel of the correct length might be dug to allow his troops to enter. The story is couched in legendary terms, but Needham, whose judgment in these matters is to be relied on, is not prepared to dismiss it entirely.

Kites seem to have been used for various military purposes during the first millennium A.D. They were used for signalling in China in the sixth and eighth centuries,[3] while in 1232 they were the means of carrying out what was probably the first leaflet raid:

> The besieged sent up paper kites with writing on them, and when these came over the northern (i.e. the Mongol) lines, the strings were cut (so that they fell among) the Chin prisoners (there). (The messages) incited them (to revolt and escape). People who saw this said: 'Only a few days ago the Chin (commanders) were using red paper lanterns (for signalling) and now they are making use of paper kites. If the generals think they can defeat the enemy by such methods they will find it very difficult.'[4]

In rather more recent times kite-flying has, of course, been indulged in principally

[1] Needham, *op. cit.*, p. 573.
[2] Laufer, *op. cit.*, p. 23.
[3] Needham, *op. cit.*, p. 577.
[4] *Ibid.*, pp. 577–8.

as a sport. According to Laufer, the use of kites as a source of amusement began no earlier than the northern Sung dynasty (A.D. 960–1126), after which it became increasingly popular. For centuries it has been traditional to fly them on 'Kites' Day', a festival held on the ninth day of the ninth month. In former times special food was consumed on this date, and there was a so-called 'literary festival', or 'festival of the ascension', which may have been associated with the traditional bureaucratic examinations held during the preceding month. A story describing the origin of the festival tells how a man called Huan Ching was informed by a fortune-teller that on the ninth day of the ninth month a great calamity would befall his house and property. He was therefore instructed to take his family into the hills on the day in question, having previously provided each person with a little red bag of pieces of dog-wood, tied to the wrist as a talisman. In the hills they were to spend their time drinking chrysanthemum-wine. Ching, having done as he was bidden, returned to his house in the evening to find that all the domestic animals were dead. The story has it that in yearly memory of this occasion the people have continued to go into the hills, taking their kites to amuse themselves. It was formerly believed that the whole year's bad luck might be avoided in this way. Apart from being a source of amusement, the kites were also said to serve as an indication of their owners' future place in the literary hierarchy or in the civil service. The higher the kite flew, the greater would be its owner's success.

In a totally different attempt to account for the origin of the festival it is stated that kites are flown to honour the memory of one Mêng Chia, who lived in the fourth century A.D., and 'of whom it is recorded that, when his hat was blown off by the wind at a picnic, he remained quite unconscious of his loss'. This charming oddity may lend some weight to Needham's suggestion (see above) that the earliest kite was a Chinese farmer's hat on the end of a string.[1]

Doolittle estimated that in his time thirty or forty thousand people were to be seen in the hills outside one town on the occasion of 'Kites' Day'. Youngsters were especially encouraged to indulge in this wholesome pastime because 'it makes them throw their heads back and open their mouths, thus getting rid of internal heat'.[2]

Chinese kites are not only beautiful and varied in form, but are also commonly

[1] De Groot, J. J. M., *Les Fêtes annuellement célébrées à Emoui*, Paris, 1886, Pt. 2, pp. 530–7; Doolittle, Rev. J., *Social Life of the Chinese*, 2 vols., London, 1866, Vol. 2, p. 70; Williams, C. A. S., *Encyclopedia of Chinese Symbolism and Art Motives*, New York, 1960, p. 14.

[2] Laufer, *op. cit.*, p. 36; De Groot, *op. cit.*, p. 537.

equipped with simple musical instruments which are operated by the force of the wind. A famous tenth century kite-maker, Li Yeh, is said to have invented some of the earliest musical kites by fitting a sort of Aeolian harp to the structure. Metal strings stretched across an aperture are caused to vibrate in the wind. Kites made in this way are called 'wind psalteries' – a term commonly used as a name for any kite. Others are equipped with whistles or pan-pipes. Li Yeh is sometimes credited with having invented the wind-pipe kite also, but this seems to have existed much earlier. Laufer quotes a story referring to the Han (began 202 B.C.):

> During the reign of the emperor Liu Pang, the founder of the Han dynasty, a general who was much attached to the dynasty which had been obliged to give way before the more powerful house of Han, resolved to make a last vigorous effort to drive Liu Pang from the throne he had recently usurped. A battle, however, resulted in the army of the general being hemmed in and threatened with annihilation. At his wit's end to devise a method of escape, he at last conceived the ingenious idea of frightening the enemy by flying kites, fitted with Aeolian strings, over their camp in the dead of night. The wind was favorable, and when all was wrapt in darkness and silence, the forces of Liu Pang heard sounds in the air resembling *Fu Han!* Beware of Han! It was their guardian angels, they declared, who were warning them of impending danger, and they precipitately fled, hotly pursued by the general and his army.[1]

There is no doubt that kites in China were often built large enough to bear a man aloft. (The huge Japanese kites still built in recent times provide a clear indication of the capacity of oriental peoples to carry out this feat with no difficulty.) The Chinese man-lifters were apparently sometimes used for military observation posts, but there is no evidence to suggest that flying from a kite was ever indulged in for pleasure. Indeed, such flights are of course highly dangerous, and their danger seems to have been well appreciated. Needham quotes examples of enforced kite-flying as punishment,[2] while both he and Lynn White independently recognized a reference by Marco Polo to a special form of manned kite.[3] Polo's detailed description is of the utmost interest:

> And so we will tell you how, when any ship must go on a voyage, they prove whether its business will go well or ill on that voyage. The men of the ship indeed

[1] Laufer, *op. cit.*, p. 34.
[2] Needham, *op. cit.*, pp. 587–9.
[3] *Ibid.*, p. 589.

will have a hurdle, that is a grating, of withies, and at each corner and side of the hurdle will be tied a cord, so that there will be eight cords, and they will all be tied at the other end with a long rope. Again they will find someone stupid or drunken and will bind him on the hurdle; for no wise man nor undepraved would expose himself to that danger. And this is done when a strong wind prevails. They indeed set up the hurdle opposite the wind, and the wind lifts the hurdle and carries it into the sky and the men hold on by the long rope. And if while it is in the air the hurdle leans towards the way of the wind [Lat. 'uersus cursum uenti declinet'], they pull the rope to them a little and then the hurdle is set upright, and they let out some rope and the hurdle rises. And if it leans down again they pull the rope by so much till the hurdle is set up and rises, and they let out some rope; so that in this way it would rise so much that it could not be seen, if only the rope should be so long. This proof is made in this way, namely that if the hurdle going straight up makes for the sky, they say that the ship for which that proof has been made will make a quick and prosperous voyage, and all the merchants run together to her for the sake of sailing and going with her. And if the hurdle has not been able to go up, no merchant will be willing to enter the ship for which the proof was made, because they say that she could not finish her voyage and many ills would oppress her. And so that ship stays in port that year.[1]

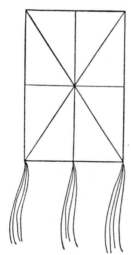

Fig. 1.
Probable shape of the
earliest Chinese kites

It is plain that Marco Polo had never seen a kite before (see Chapter 4), but any practised kite-flier will find his account of the manipulation of the line very convincing. Furthermore, his description of the kite itself ('a grating, of withies') would

[1] Polo, M., *The Description of the World*, 2 vols., ed. A. C. Moule and P. Pelliot, London, 1938, Vol. 1, pp. 356–7.

be perfectly appropriate to that other great eastern kite of man-lifting proportions: the Japanese *wan-wan* (see Fig. 15).

(Marco Polo's account, included only in the rare 'Z' manuscript, would of course have had no effect on the development of the kite in Europe, even if it had been widely read. It was just another oriental curiosity.)

Since they were made for practical rather than for aesthetic purposes, the earliest Chinese kites appear to have been built in simple rectangular form (Fig. 1). Kites of this general configuration are seen most frequently in the early illustrations, and

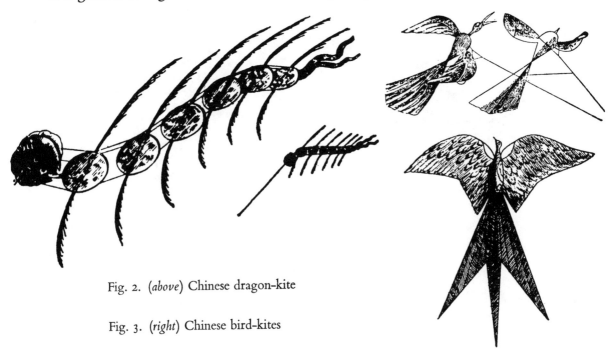

Fig. 2. (*above*) Chinese dragon-kite

Fig. 3. (*right*) Chinese bird-kites

further evidence may be adduced from the Korean and Japanese designs. Kites seem to have reached Korea during the first millennium A.D. (see Chapter 2), after which there appears to have been very little modification of their design. The shape of the typical Korean kite is illustrated in Fig. 6. Japanese kites, which also derive from Chinese models, seem originally to have been of the rectangular type.

While the Korean kite has remained virtually unchanged, both Chinese and Japanese kites have been developed in various ways, so that a great many complex and sophisticated shapes now coexist with the plain rectangle of earlier times. Recent Chinese kites are too numerous to list in full. They include figure-kites, bird-kites (and various other winged figures), and the spectacular dragon or centipede kites (Figs. 2, 3). The last, which are sometimes sixty or more feet in length, are composed of a series of circular or elliptical discs (each acting independently as a kite). The discs are joined by two or more lines which keep them flying parallel, no matter what their angle to the wind. (This system was later adopted by certain western kite-designers who developed man-lifters (see Chapter 7).) At the front is an ornamental dragon's head which may include revolving eyes and even a smoke-producing

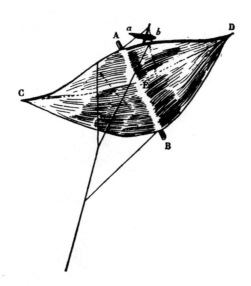

Fig. 4. Typical Chinese kite with
hummer attached

Fig. 5. Typical figure-kite

mouth. Several points of attachment are usually necessary in order to bridle the dragon effectively, and a whole team of men may be needed to launch and fly it.

The bird kites are rendered stable by means of the concave pockets in their wings, and by a certain amount of flexibility which enables them to adjust to wind pressure. (A further winged kite, of Japanese design, but similar to the Chinese version, is depicted in Fig. 13.)

A great deal has been said about the extreme skill necessary in order to fly Chinese kites successfully. While it is true that without a deal of practice it is far from easy to manœuvre fighting-kites (see below, p. 36), the flying of the tailless bird and figure-kites is really quite simple. Any western kite enthusiast is likely to find that they are much easier to handle than the common tailed kite flown by children.

THE DISTRIBUTION OF THE EASTERN KITE BEFORE A.D. 1600

Soon after its appearance in China the kite spread to neighbouring countries (see map). Japan took it over, together with so much else from Chinese culture; it was soon familiar to the Koreans; and it spread south and west into Burma, the Malayan peninsula, Indonesia, and India. The date of the spread is uncertain, but the kite seems to have been known in the Malayan area for at least two thousand years. It passed very early into the culture of Polynesia, as far east as Easter Island, though it was perhaps not known during the earliest stages of the Polynesian settlements. As is discussed in Chapter 4, it made its way across southern Asia into Arabia, perhaps as much as 1,500 years ago. With the possible exception of the further spread indicated by the broken lines on the map, that was as far afield as the kite travelled before the expansion of European civilization.

It appears to have been unknown on the American continent. There is no mention of it in Stewart Culin's monumental *Games of the North American Indians*,[1] and Mr Thor Heyerdahl tells me[2] that he is unaware of any evidence of its existence elsewhere in America. The latter fact is substantial confirmation, since Mr Heyerdahl's purposes would have been very well served if the contrary could have been demonstrated.

There appears to be no evidence of the kite's early existence on the other continents. Hans Plischke[3] mentions a sighting in Australia, but an examination of his source shows that an indigenous kite is not in question. His reference concerns a kite flown by children of European descent.

Though the kite may at one time have been universally known in Oceania (a point about which there is no certainty), it has since progressively died out. Native Polynesian kites ceased to be made in New Zealand about a century ago, and even before the coming of the white man they seem to have disappeared from a

[1] Washington, 1907.
[2] Private letter, dated August 17, 1965.
[3] Plischke, H., *Der Fischdrachen*, Leipzig, 1922, p. 35.

number of Pacific centres, such as Samoa, Tonga, Fiji, and New Caledonia. The reason for the disappearance of the kite from these areas appears to be wholly unknown.

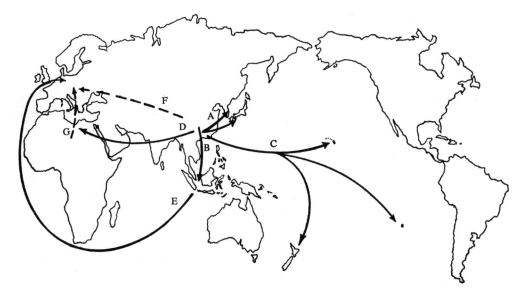

THE DISTRIBUTION OF THE EASTERN KITE BEFORE A.D. 1600

A. To Korea and Japan.
B. To the Malay Archipelago.
C. Throughout Oceania, as far east as Easter Island.
D. Through Burma and India, to Arabia and North Africa.
E. To Europe, via the ocean-going trade routes.
F. Possible reinsemination during the Mongol invasions.
G. Probable importations from European contact with Arabia.

1. Chinese children flying kites. From a scroll attributed to Su Han-Ch'en (Sung period), but probably later. *Chicago Natural History Museum*

2. Kite-flying at Hae-Kwan, early 19th century. (After Wright's *China*.)

3. Small Chinese dragon kite.

4. Chinese figure kites of modern
construction. *Smithsonian Institution*

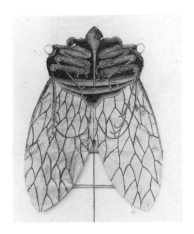

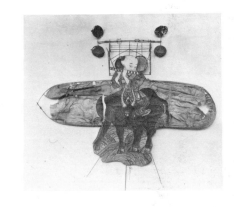

5a, b. Japanese man-lifter, *ca.* 1860.

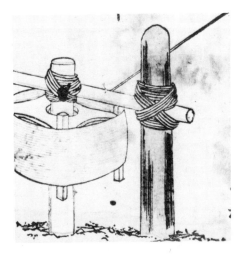

5c. Winch for the man-lifter in Plates 5a, b.

6. Giant *wan-wan* kite ready to fly, 1906.

7. Malaysian *wau bulan* kites.

8. Malaysian *wau bulan* kite.

9. Malaysian figure kite.

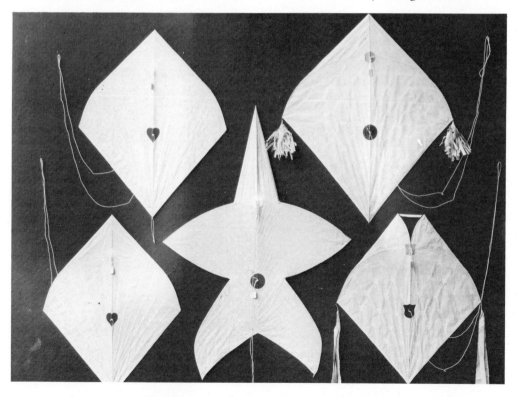

10. Thai kites. The centre one is a *chula*, that in the bottom right-hand corner is a musical kite, while the others—versions of the Nagasaki fighting kite—are *pakpao*.

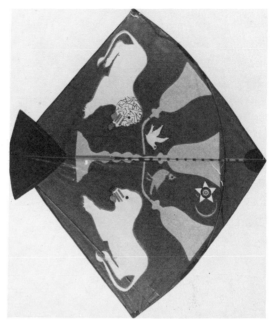

11, 12. Indian fighting kites.

13. Fishing kites. A spider web lure is attached to the one on the left. *University Museum of Archaeology and Ethnology, Cambridge*

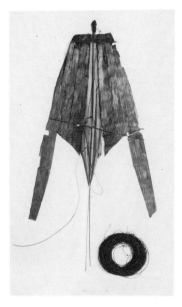

14. Fishing kites. (a) and (b) are from the Solomons, (c) is from Dobu. Lengths respectively 48 in., 31.75 in., 26.5 in. *British Museum*

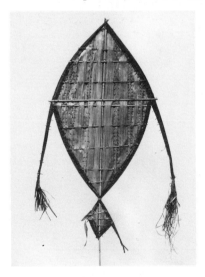

15. Banks Island kite. Apparently intended to represent a fish. Length 45.5 in. *British Museum*

16. Maori bird-kite from the East Cape District. 138.5 in. X 51 in. *Auckland Museum*

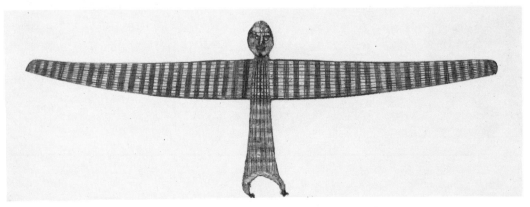
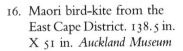

2 | Other Eastern Kites

Space does not permit the inclusion of a detailed survey of all the kites and kite-customs of the many eastern countries in which the sport is popular. Such a survey would itself fill several volumes. Instead, I have provided, in this chapter, a brief summary of kite-flying in a few selected places where the kites are of more than usual interest.

I have myself flown a number of eastern kites and can testify to the beautiful performance of such designs as the Nagasaki kite, the Chinese and Japanese winged and bird-kites, the fast Korean fighting-kite, and the amusing snake-kites from Cambodia. The flying of kites of indigenous design for contests and even, in many cases, for private pleasure is, however, a fast dying pastime in many parts of Asia and the Pacific. Amusements of a more modern character are taking its place and even when kites are still flown they tend to be strongly influenced by the west. (No one, for example, would use fibre cord when nylon line is available.) It is not easy to obtain information on the state of an art so relatively neglected in recent times in so many different parts of the world, some of which are at present virtually closed to the western investigator. For these reasons I have in most cases described kite-festivals and the like in the past tense, unless I have very good reason to know that they are still regularly and vigorously taking place. The death of indigenous kite-flying in many countries is a matter of no doubt whatever–Maori bird-kites, for example, are regrettably extinct–but I apologize in advance to the reader if in other cases I have prematurely, and through ignorance, announced the demise of the art.

KOREA

As mentioned earlier, Korean kites were in fact imported from China, but, as elsewhere in the Orient, there are in Korea a number of local stories purporting to account for their origin. One such concerns a riot of farmers which took place during the Goryo Dynasty (A.D. 918–1380). A famous general, Choe Yong, was sent to subdue the rebels. He travelled by water, but found when he arrived at the stronghold that precipitous cliffs made a landing impossible. He used his ingenuity to construct a kite which carried fire over the enemy walls, or, according to a somewhat more fanciful version of the story, carried men into the stronghold.

Another story, from an earlier period, concerns General Gim Yu-Sin (A.D. 595–673). Choe Sang-Su tells it in charming oriental English:

> In the first year of Queen Zindong, the 28th ruler of the Silla Dynasty, there was a revolt by Bi-dam and Yom-zong Gim Yu-Sin, a famous general undertook a mission to subdue the rebels. During this military operation, one evening, it happened that a large star suddenly appeared and fell toward the earth near the castle named Wol-song (a palace of the Silla Dynasty). It was generally believed in those days that a falling star was a very bad omen, especially during wartime. It meant that terrible bloodshed and disaster would come. So the people and soldiers began to feel uneasy. To make the situation worse, rumours went around that where the star had fallen terrible bloodshed would ensue and their queen would be defeated. This made the people and the soldiers extremely nervous and uneasy. It seemed to be very difficult to control the agitated public. General Gim Yu-Sin thought that he had to find some means of carrying a fireball high up in the sky, and let it disappear. A kite could carry a fireball from ground to the sky. One evening a fireball going up into the sky was seen by the people who finally thought that the fallen star had gone back to heaven. With the soldiers' morale boosted, General Gim Yu-Sin was able to control the public and destroy the rebels.[1]

The early Korean kites were said to be of considerable size, but the great majority of modern examples are no more than two or three feet long, though in some cases they may reach as much as five feet. They are made exclusively of bamboo and paper (Fig. 6).

The diameter of the centre hole is about one-third of the length of the spine. The top horizontal stick is bowed back and a three-leg bridle is attached to the top

[1] Choe Sang-Su, *The Survey of Korean Kites*, Seoul, 1958, p. 3.

corners and to a point on the spine midway between the centre and the bottom. A fourth string, more loosely tied, runs from the junction of the bridle strings to the centre of the kite. This prevents undue buckling in a strong wind. The triangular 'feet' of paper are optional. When it is used as a fighting-kite, no tail is attached. It is a very fast mover.

Although this is the standard kite, a number of other shapes are sometimes flown. These include a 'crown' kite (a variant of the standard), a 'tiger' (in the form of the Chinese character for tiger), a cross-shaped kite, and a version of the Nagasaki fighting-kite (see p. 39).

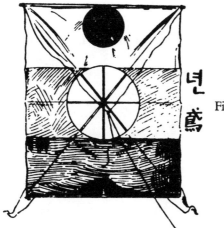

Fig. 6. Korean kite

In recent times kites have been flown in Korea almost exclusively for kite-fighting contests, but it seems that they were once used for ceremonial purposes. Choe Sang-Su writes:

> We find that there were many national celebration days during the period of the Three Kingdoms . . . On these national celebration days, people from all over the country gathered in front of an altar to offer the national sacrifices to heaven. It was customary after the ceremony for the people who had gathered either in front of the altar or on a nearby plain to watch various displays, of which kite flying was one.[1]

[1] *Ibid.*, p. 6.

In modern Korea, kites are flown at only one season: during the first two weeks of the year. The main contest is a 'kite-fight' which involves trying to sever another man's line by crossing it with one's own and giving a rapid tug. The line near the kite is sharpened for this purpose by passing it several times through a mixture of glue and powdered glass or porcelain. This form of kite-fighting which is widespread throughout the Orient may, like the kite itself, have originated in China. Choe, once again, provides a description:

> The paramount game in kite flying is the engagement of kite strings, usually two at a time. One of the strings is doomed to be broken off by the sawing effect of the friction between the two strings. The kite drifts away and its string falls to the ground. The loser has to have his reel rolling fast to save as much of his string as he can, while youngsters are eagerly waiting for the string to fall on the ground so that they can snatch pieces of it for themselves. Youngsters are so eager to follow after the drifting kite that they often fall into ditches or dirty water as they run looking into the sky to follow after the drifting kite's course. Anybody can catch a drifting kite which has been conquered in such an engagement. It usually happens that youngsters running for a drifting kite climb over neighbor's house fence, roofs, or gardens or climb up a high tree where the drifting kite has been caught. . . . When a string is cut and the kite starts drifting, the shouts of excitement are intense.[1]

Such contests tended to become less popular during the Sino-Japanese war, but in later years President Syngman Rhee revived interest, largely by taking part himself. Kites are either made by the contestants or bought from kite-merchants who are a familiar sight all over the Orient. The most expensive part of the equipment is, or was, the line, which was traditionally of silk and could be had in a variety of colours. Culin tells us that in his time the line used for kites at the Royal Palace was sky blue.[2]

The Korean kite is designed to be only marginally stable. The flier keeps it up by careful manipulation of the line, which is conveniently wound on a reel. (The flier holds the reel, rather than the line itself.) By pulling and releasing at the appropriate times, the kite can be made to move in any desired direction—even to windward. (This is a characteristic of any fighting-kite.) Choe claims that the Korean kite is faster than that of any other country, but in my experience the Nagasaki kite is superior (see below, p. 39).

[1] *Ibid.*, p. 10.
[2] Culin, S., *Korean Games*, Philadelphia, 1895, p. 11.

Kite contests, as one would expect, are exclusively male affairs. Women are, however, said to fly kites occasionally from the back-yards of their houses. According to Choe, anyone can tell from its movement whether a kite is being flown by a woman. Certainly the utmost dexterity is required to put a Korean kite through all the evolutions of which it is capable.

On the fifteenth day of the year, when the kite-flying season ends, the 'kite for warding off evil' is flown. This is an ordinary kite on which are written the words 'Bad luck away, good luck stay'. The flier attaches a tail (to make the kite fly steadily without continuous control from the ground), launches it from a hill, and, when all the line is out, releases both kite and line. (According to Culin, boys used sometimes to attach a piece of sulphur-paper to the line, which, after igniting, burned through the line and released the kite. In this way the expensive line was saved.) By virtue of the kite's disappearance the flier is symbolically relieved of his burden of ill-luck. Anyone seeing an abandoned kite will let it lie, since otherwise he would become a victim of the other man's misfortunes.

JAPAN

It has been suggested that the kite was introduced into Japan by the Indians who accompanied the Deshima Dutch, but it was certainly known in that country for centuries before then, and must have been introduced from China. Although in China the kite seems to have begun as a technological object of mainly practical significance, there are hints to suggest that in Japan it rapidly acquired some ceremonial and religious value. Kites and paintings of kites are found associated with temples and with a number of tales of religious character, while more recently the *wan-wan* (see below) had a tinge of religious awe about it. This did not, however, prevent the Japanese from making, even in the earliest times, as much practical use of kites as did their Chinese predecessors. It is said, for example, that the twelfth-century hero Minamoto no Tametomo sent his son from Oshima to Kamakura by means of a kite.[1]

There are Japanese chronicles telling of the use of kites in warfare to fly men into and out of beleaguered cities, and to provide observation-posts in the manner independently suggested centuries later by western experimenters with military kites

[1] For this story and a number of other tales, see Müller, W., *Der Papierdrachen in Japan*, Stuttgart, 1914. Müller's little book is a most valuable first-hand account of Japanese kite-customs.

(see Chapter 10). In view of the immense size of traditional Japanese kites still flown in recent times, these stories may be treated as far from fanciful. Some three hundred years ago, indeed, a Shogun was forced to forbid the construction of giant kites after a daring adventurer had used one to invade his palace. Another adventurer brought about a further ban on large kites some years later. This was the famous robber Ishikawa Goyemon, who used a great kite to fly up to the golden dolphins which adorned the tower of Nagoya Castle. According to one of several versions of the story, he was successful in reaching the dolphins, but managed to steal only the fins. The exploit did not benefit him very much: together with his family he was boiled in oil after his capture. (As a consequence of this robbery the dolphins were surrounded, it is said, by iron cages, but later someone nevertheless managed to steal some other parts of them.)

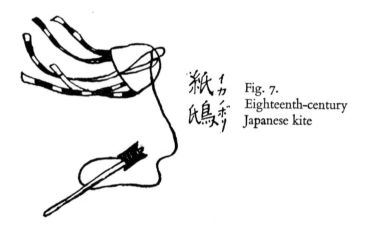

紙 イ
 カ

氏鳥 ボ
  ツ

Fig. 7.
Eighteenth-century
Japanese kite

Rather less spectacular, but more practical, was another Japanese application of the kite dating from several centuries ago: it is said that architects building complex structures sometimes used kites to carry bricks to the workmen.

Fig. 7, an illustration drawn from a book published in Japan in 1712, is reproduced from Culin.[1] As its shape makes understandable, Japanese kites are sometimes known by the words for either octopus or cuttlefish. E. S. Morse[2] describes a Tokyo kite-shop which delighted him by displaying as an advertising sign a huge cloth-covered model of a cuttlefish slowly waving its arms in the wind.

[1] Culin, *op. cit.*, p. 13.
[2] Morse, E. S., *Japan Day by Day*, Tokyo, 1936. See Part 2, *passim.*

Despite the 'cuttlefish' idea, Japanese kites nowadays vary greatly in design. The earliest were probably rectangular, like their Chinese originals, and several forms of rectangular kite are still common in Japan today, especially in the Tokyo area. Figs. 8 and 9 show the construction of two such kites. The 'war kite', with its fourteen-leg bridle, varies from six to fifteen feet in height and requires a tail. The simpler rectangular kite is much smaller (about two feet), and is sometimes equipped with a buzzer or hummer. It also requires a tail.

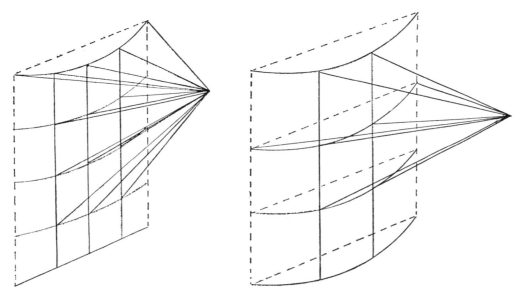

Fig. 8. Japanese 'war kite'   Fig. 9. Small Japanese rectangular kite

As in China, the simple rectangle was rapidly transformed into many other shapes. Some of the innumerable Japanese figure-kites are represented in Figs. 10–13. A great deal of symbolism is included both in the design of the kites and in their decoration. They are made to represent animals, heroes, deities, and various well known objects, and they often bear calligraphic inscriptions. (The forms are not merely traditional but are kept up to date with the addition of such modern shapes as that of the aeroplane.)

The Nagasaki kite is probably the finest fighting-kite ever designed (Fig. 14). It can be made to fly without a tail and moves with great speed in any direction. The size varies, but it is rarely more than a yard long. The best Nagasaki kites are made

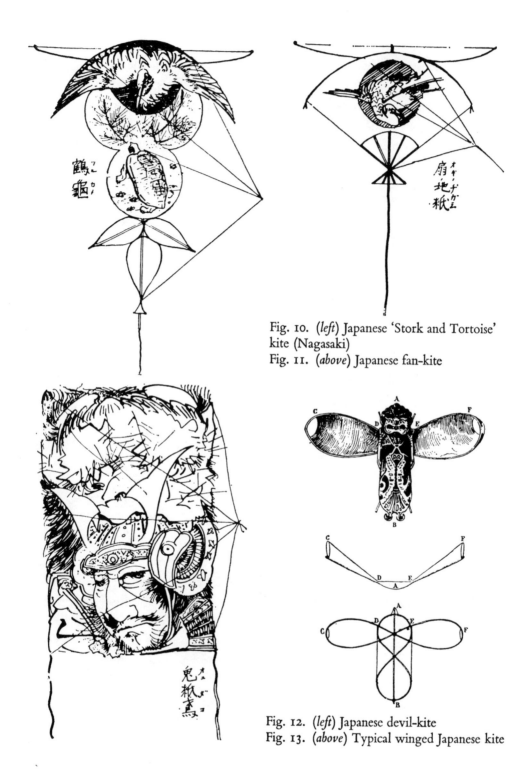

Fig. 10. (*left*) Japanese 'Stork and Tortoise'
kite (Nagasaki)
Fig. 11. (*above*) Japanese fan-kite

Fig. 12. (*left*) Japanese devil-kite
Fig. 13. (*above*) Typical winged Japanese kite

with a carefully tapered horizontal spar, and are outlined with thin thread before the paper is attached. If they are to be manœuvrable in any direction they must be very delicately balanced and perfectly symmetrical. The kites commonly flown by children are somewhat different from the best fighting variety used by adults. Their outer edges are not stiffened with thread and, in order to make flying easier, they are often provided with tails consisting of bunches of paper streamers a few feet in length. Morse has some interesting descriptions of the Nagasaki boys' habit of flying their kites from bridges. As an aid to control they often attached their lines to the ends of long bamboo poles, so anticipating the common modern technique of flying from a fishing rod.[1] He tells us also that the boys used frequently to send up mess-

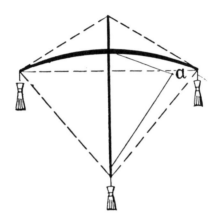

Fig. 14.
Structure of
the Nagasaki fighting-kite

engers, which, in Japan, are commonly called 'monkeys', from their shape, though sometimes they are also cut to resemble spiders or umbrellas.

The Nagasaki kite is called *hata*, meaning 'flag'. This seems to be due to its being commonly coloured red, white, and blue – the colours of the Dutch flag, from which its decorations derive. This fact raises the question of the kite's origin. It is known not only in Japan, but also in Indonesia, India, and a number of other places in south-east Asia. Sometimes the design is identical with that seen in Nagasaki, but in a few cases there are minor variations, such as the addition, in India, of the attractive fish-tail (Plates 11, 12).

It has been supposed that the Japanese copied the colours from the flags which they saw at the Dutch trading-post in Nagasaki. It is possible, however, that not only the decoration, but the kite itself, was introduced by the Dutch. I have been unable

[1] *Ibid.*, p. 142.

to obtain any firm information as to the earliest appearance in Japan of this form of kite, but it is significant that the same design, as used in the Dutch East Indies, was also decorated with the Dutch colours and was known by a name meaning 'tri-coloured flag'.[1] Furthermore, the Nagasaki kite is very different in design from almost all other Japanese kites. Until an earlier date can be established for the appearance of the fighting-kite in Nagasaki, it would seem most reasonable to suppose that the Dutch introduced the design from the Indies, together with its ready-made patriotic decorations.

Few kite-flying nations have been so possessed as the Japanese by the desire to build larger and larger kites. In the eighteenth century fliers were already having to borrow ships' tow-ropes in order to have lines of sufficient strength, and in the early nineteenth century some young people in Okazaki formed a society for the further development of the kite. Throughout the nineteenth century kites increased in size until, towards its end, the master kite-maker Nagajima Gempei developed a new constructional technique which resulted in the amazing *wan-wan* kite of Tokushima (on Shikoku). Up to 150 men might be needed to launch and fly one. Müller describes a *wan-wan*, made in 1906, which was twenty yards across and flew a tail 480 feet long. It weighed some 55 hundredweight and needed a 35-leg bridle. Such kites could not, of course, be built and owned by individuals but were the property of the whole population of a district, who were summoned to bouts of kite-building by the ringing of temple bells. The *wan-wan*, which was bowed back to produce stability, was constructed of bamboo spars twelve inches in circumference, and was covered with hundreds of sheets of a special tough paper. Launching, of course, was not easy. The kite was placed against a large trestle (Fig. 15) and a team of men heaved on the line. Such kites were so big that once they were launched it was often impossible to bring them in, in which case they were left to fall of their own accord when the wind eased, though this usually destroyed them.

Kite-flying festivals are still held in Japan, but they were once much more common and more spectacular. Müller describes the festivals which were held in his time (*ca.* 1910), after the fliers had been driven out of the cities into the fields by the many networks of power-lines which had begun to cover the country. He found tens of thousands of people delightedly taking part. Booths were set up around the contest area and large quantities of food and *sake* were consumed.

[1] Dewall, H. A., 'Het Vliegerspel te Batavia', *Tijdschrift voor Indische Taal-, Land- en Volken-kunde*, Vol. 50, 1908, p. 423.

In Nagasaki the main sport was kite-fighting of the type described above in connexion with Korean kites. Before Japan was opened to the west, however, the powdered glass used to sharpen the cutting lines was difficult to procure. Müller says that the Japanese would pay very high prices to the Deshima Dutch for old broken bottles and other discarded glassware. If glass was unprocurable, sand and powdered porcelain might be used as substitutes.

In other parts of the country where kite-fighting is still practised, fliers use a different method of cutting down an opposing kite. Instead of the sharpened line,

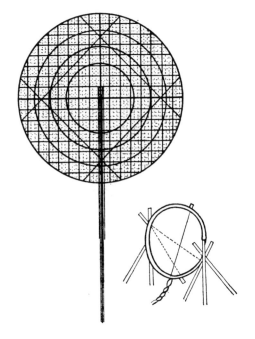

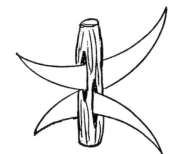

Fig. 16. Knives for kite-fighting

Fig. 15. Structure of the *wan-wan* kite and its launching trestle

knives of various sorts (called 'gangiri') are attached to the kites. Curved knife-blades are pushed through slits in a piece of bamboo, which is then tied immediately below the kite (Fig. 16). In other places no cutting tool is used, but the flier attempts to sever the opponent's line by means of friction alone.

Japanese children, in common with others in the east, like to furnish their kites with 'hummers' consisting of taut bow-strings which vibrate in the wind, or of taut lengths of whalebone, sheet brass, or raw-hide. Such hummers are normally attached only to small kites, and sometimes, as in China, several are fitted to the one kite so that a harmony is produced.

The subject of Japanese kites cannot be left without mention of the celebration of the Boys' Festival, on May 5. In some areas, such as Sagami and Suruga, large seven-sided kites used to be flown. These were occasionally as much as eighteen feet long and not infrequently one or two members of the kite-team would allow themselves to be raised from the ground. The event caused so much excitement and consequent damage to property that the police had finally to restrain these age-old festivities.

At the Boys' Festival there is also a widespread custom of flying quasi-kites which are really windsocks in the form of carp, recalling the hollow dragons of mediæval Europe (see Chapter 4). The following description is found in Culin:

> The 5th of May is marked by a festival . . . in honor of boys, the girls already having had their day, on the 3d of March. It is celebrated in every house which has been favored with the advent of a boy baby during the previous twelve months, and, to a less extent, in houses where there are boys below the age of seven. In front of the door are set up flags bearing the family crest, figures of warriors, elephants, tigers, dragons, and so forth. The most conspicuous object, however, is a tall pole, generally surrounded by a round basket, covered with gilding, and having attached to it long narrow streamers, and a little wheel turned by the wind. From these poles, bellying out in the breeze, are one, or two, or three large-sized colored carp, made of cloth or paper. The carp being a fish which resolutely overcomes all difficulties it encounters in its passage up the streams of the country, even ascending waterfalls, and eventually, it is said, being changed into a flying dragon, it is chosen to shadow forth what it is hoped will be the career of any youthful male members of the household. Inside the house, small flags and a military ensign, *umajirushi*, are set up in a wooden frame, together with helmets, and figures of fighting men, all being expressions of the hope that the small boys of the house may ultimately become great men. Old books say that the holiday was observed as far back as the reign of Jintoku Tenno, about fifteen centuries ago.[1]

MALAYA AND INDONESIA

Kite-flying has been practised for so long in Malaya that many people have believed it to have originated there. Some form of kite–perhaps the leaf-shaped fishing-kites (see Chapter 3)–may well have been independently invented some-

---

[1] Culin, *op. cit.*, p. 19n.

where in the area. There appears unfortunately to be little written evidence from the earliest times, but by the fifteenth century kites were so well established that contests were documented in the Malay Annals.

Nowadays most Malayan kites are made of bamboo (particularly a variety called *buloh duri*) and of a thin stiff paper which was originally alien to the country, but there are other kites, of less sophisticated design, which are still made of sewn leaves. It appears that the early Malayan kites were all made in the latter way. Only after the sixteenth century was paper introduced for kite-making.

A variety of shapes is now used, most of them being bowed and capable of flying without tails. There are so-called Cat, Peacock, Swallow, Fish, Frog, Man, and

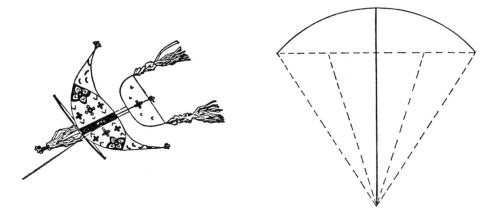

Fig. 17. Humming kite from Kelantan (Malaya)   Fig. 18. Malayan arch-top kite

Western kites (the last being of Thai origin). The most generally popular, and most typically Malayan shape is the 'moon' kite, or *wau bulan*, the hinder part of which is shaped like a new moon (Plate 7). This is the kite normally used in contests. It is a magnificent flier, the ellipsoidal plan of the main wing being aerodynamically very satisfactory.

A variant of this kite from Kelantan (north-east Malaya), where the pastime is especially popular, is illustrated in Fig. 17. These kites are gaily decorated with charms and designs of conventional Malay type, and streamers of coloured paper are attached to the nose and at the wing-tips. The average length is about five feet, but some are as long as ten feet. As shown in the illustrations, they are often built with a hummer, which fosters the legend that the kites come to life once they are aloft.

According to Kijang Puteh[1] the manufacture of a first-class specimen of *wau bulan* may occupy a man for three weeks, working eight hours a day.

A simpler form of Malayan kite is illustrated in Fig. 18. This is strikingly like the common English arch-top kite and bears a close resemblance to the Javanese pear-kite (see below). It is flown from a two-leg bridle attached to top and bottom.

Various kinds of contest are held, usually in *padi* fields after harvest. There are competitions for highest flier, best decoration, loudest hum, etc., the prize usually being a piece of cloth or a sarong. Kite-fights similar to those described in the sections on Korea and Japan are occasionally held, but due to ill-feeling which these sometimes produce, they were banned some years ago in Kota Bharu. According to D. F. A. Hervey[2] the Malayan cutting strings for such contests are sometimes made by passing the string through a mixture of ground glass and sago.

Sometimes, if the wind is strong and the moon is clear, the kites are left flying all night so that the pleasant humming may lull their owners to sleep, while a change in pitch may serve as a storm-warning.

Kite-flying is no less popular in Indonesia. As is mentioned above, a fighting-kite identical with the Nagasaki kite is well known there. A full description of kite contests in Batavia is given in an article by H. A. Dewall.[3] The adult contests make use of the familiar sharpened line, but Dewall describes fights by children which involve simply trying to knock the opponent's kite out of the sky.

Dewall divides the Batavian kites with which he was familiar into three categories: (1) the fighting-kites; (2) children's kites similar to the European diamond; (3) 'luxury-kites', which are for show only. The last category includes figure-kites representing men, animals, and objects, and also 'humming kites' similar to the Malayan kites described above.

Woglom[4] describes further Indonesian kites, flown in Java in the nineteenth century. One of these is identical with the European pear-kite (see Fig. 54), which lends weight to the theory that kites reached Europe largely due to Portuguese, Dutch, and English contacts with the Indies (see p. 62). Another is the original form of the kite from which Eddy took the hint for his familiar 'bow kite' (also known

[1] Kijang Puteh, 'Malay Kites', *Straits Times Annual*, 1962, pp. 8–11.
[2] Hervey, D. F. A., 'Malay Games', *Journal of the Anthropological Institute of Great Britain and Ireland*, Vol. 33, 1903, pp. 291–2.
[3] Dewall, *op. cit.*
[4] Woglom, G. T., *Parakites*, New York, 1896, Chapter I.

in the west as the 'Malay' kite). In essentials this kite differs from Eddy's only in the bridle and in the lower cross-over point of the sticks (Fig. 19).

From Indonesia there comes another object which may perhaps have some bearing on the development of the kite. In parts of the Philippines the rice-crops are protected from the possible depredations of small birds by the use of large imitation birds made of bamboo. These are suspended from the top of a pole erected in the field. The smaller birds, seeing the large bamboo imitations moving around in the wind, are frightened away by what they take to be an enemy. Although the bamboo birds are in no sense kites, they are sufficiently similar to suggest that they may be either cognate or related. The effigies, the wings of which are woven in a manner

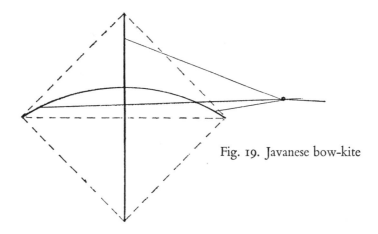

Fig. 19. Javanese bow-kite

recalling the construction of the Maori kites, may perhaps be degenerate relics of once fully functional kites. In other parts of the world genuine kites have frequently been used for similar purposes. (See Chapter 10.)

THAILAND

Among the south-east Asian countries Thailand has perhaps been the most devoted to kite-flying. Indeed, kite-flying has traditionally been referred to as the national pastime of the country. There, as elsewhere in Asia and the Pacific, kites seem originally to have had a magical and ceremonial significance. They were flown, in particular, in order to encourage the north-east monsoon. G. E. Gerini comments that in the Ayudhya period 'large paper kites were flown with the object of calling up the seasonal wind by the fluttering noise they made. The festival, which took place in the first month . . . was obviously connected with husbandry, as the wind prevailing at this season is the north-east monsoon, which when beginning to blow, sweeps the rain clouds away, so that fine weather sets in and the yearly flood quickly abates, the fields drying rapidly'.[1]

It seems that in past centuries kites were flown for long periods, a roster of mandarins being detailed to keep them up. La Loubère, in his famous book on Siam, translated into English in 1693,[2] writes that the kite 'of the King of Siam is in the Air every Night for the two Winter-months, and some Mandarins are nominated to ease one another in holding the String'. Each Thai mandarin is said, besides, to have been provided with his own special kite, with special colours, rather like the banners of European knights.

More recently, an annual kite-festival has been held on the Royal Cremation Ground, attended by the King and members of the Royal Family. Kite-fights between individuals and general competitions for beauty and originality have both been held, the kites in all cases being made of paper and bamboo.

An article by W. R. Moore[3] describes modern kite-festivals in Thailand: 'The long Phramane is divided across the middle with a bamboo barrier. On one side, downwind, scores of small kites are sent up; from the opposite side large star-shaped male kites are flown.

'Riding on hundreds of feet of cord, the male kites invade the territory in which the smaller ones are flying. The idea of the competition is for the large male kite to fight and entangle the others and then try to haul a victim back over the dividing line.

'Kite operators manipulate the kites with remarkable skill. The big stars soar and plunge, seeking to snare their smaller opponents. Equally skilful, the small kite flyers seek to avoid the big kite or to bring it down in their own territory. For such a catch the small kite handler gets as prize twice the sum that the male kite operator gets for any victory he may win.'

The male kite (called *chula*), on whose string small spurs are attached for catching

---

[1] Gerini, G. E., 'Festivals and Fasts (Siamese)', in Hastings' *Encyclopedia of Religions and Ethics*, Vol. 5, p. 888.

[2] La Loubère, S. de, *Historical Relation of the Kingdom of Siam*, London, 1693, p. 49.

[3] Moore, W. R., 'Scintillating Siam', *The National Geographic Magazine*, Vol. 91, No. 2, February 1947, pp. 194, 197.

the opponents' strings, is shaped like a typical oriental bird-kite (Plate 10). The female kite is called *pakpao*.

Another form of contest involves the flying of a kite through a loop attached to a second kite – an operation calling for great skill in manœuvring.

I have been able to find only very casual mention of kites in the Thai literature which was available to me, but Wales[1] quotes an old Siamese legend of a lover's being led to his lady by following the string of a runaway kite. This legend bears some similarity to many stories of runaway kites which are found in the Pacific. A further story, told in Tachard's *Second Voyage*,[2] relates how the Siamese god Sommonocodon was trying one day to fly a kite near the Palace but was prevented from doing so with any success because of the unequal height of the trees. He thereupon ordered the trees to assume an even height, which they did – and continued to do, at least until Tachard's time.

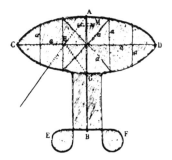

Fig. 20. Nineteenth century 'musical kite' (with hummer), from Annam.

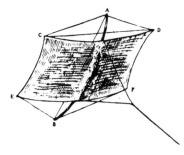

Fig. 21. So-called 'Malay kite,' designed in the 1890s by the American, J. B. Millet, and based on south-east Asian models.

[1] Wales, H. G. Q., *Siamese State Ceremonies*, London, 1931, pp. 221–2.
[2] Tachard, *Second Voyage du père Tachard*, Paris, 1689, pp. 256–7.

4

3 | The Pacific

KITE-FISHING

The spread of the kite into the Pacific from the Asiatic mainland led to an interesting practical application in some parts of Indonesia, Micronesia, Melanesia, and Polynesia. Here kites are or were used as an aid to catching gar-fish. This long-nosed fish swims very near the surface of the water and is rather timid. Its mouth is quite small, making it difficult to catch with such hooks as can be readily produced by primitive means. A modern western fisherman can catch gar-fish by trailing a very light nylon line ending in a small hook. Such a line will remain for some time on the surface of the water. The native lines, however, tending to sink rather readily, needed some form of buoyancy which would not frighten the gar-fish. The kite was used in order to overcome these difficulties.

The technique varies slightly from place to place, but is basically as follows: a kite, made of a leaf or leaves, is flown to a considerable height, sometimes from the shore, but more often from a canoe. Attached to the kite, usually at its lowest point, is another line which is allowed to hang down to the surface of the water. At the bottom of this line is a means of catching the fish. This may be a hook, but is more often either a noose of line baited with a fish or prawn (the noose catches the gar-fish by tightening around its snout), or a thick loop of spider-web two or three inches long, in which the gar-fish's jaws become entangled (Fig. 22). According to Edge-Partington,[1] up to ten fish can be caught, one after the other, with the one loop, provided it is handled carefully. Thereafter it becomes too ragged and must be replaced.

It has been suggested that one advantage of the fishing-kite lies in its acting as a

[1] Edge-Partington, T. W., 'Kite Fishing by the Salt-water Natives of Mala or Malaita Island, British Solomon Islands', *Man*, Vol. 12, 1912, pp. 9–11.

lure for the fish, which believe it to be an aquatic bird hovering over a shoal of small-fry. The gar-fish, according to the theory, approach the general area in which the small-fry are thought to be found.

In some places the kite is flown from the hand; in others the line is held in the mouth while the canoe is paddled; in still other areas the line is passed through a ring in the end of a primitive fishing-rod.

The kites used in this way vary greatly in shape and construction. Some are made of a single leaf without any additional strengthening, the lines being simply attached to appropriate points near the leaf's centre. Others are made of a single leaf strength-

Fig. 22.
Spider-web lure trailed
from a fishing-kite

ened by means of slender rods threaded through the margins. Others again are made of several leaves or strips of leaf sewn together and held rigid by means of stick-frames of varying complexity (see Fig. 23). The flying-line is attached near the top, or in some cases to a two-leg bridle running from top to bottom. No tail is needed for most fishing-kites, since the trailing fishing-line serves to steady them. Extra steadiness is achieved in some kites by means of leaf-streamers which are allowed to project from the sides.

There is no firm agreement as to where this method of fishing began, nor as to how and when it spread, but it seems likely that it was first used in the general area of the Banda Sea and that it was propagated in both easterly and westerly directions.

Kite-fishing is not, however, restricted to primitive parts of the world. It was used in England at least as long ago as 1901[1] by an enthusiastic fisherman who flew

[1] *Daily Mail* (London), September 21, 1901.

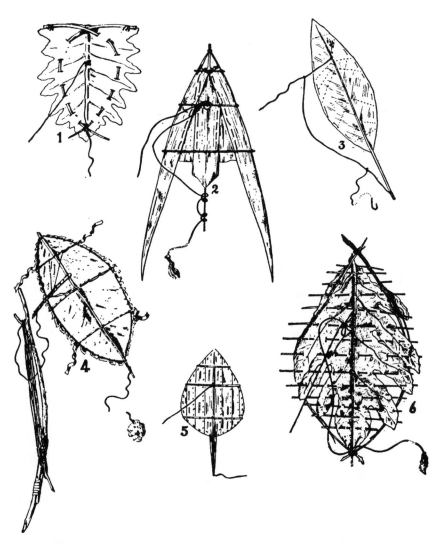

Fig. 23. Typical fishing-kites. (1) Talaut Island; (2) Solomons; (3) Banda; (4) Admiralties; (5) Marshall Bennet; (6) Oleai

two box kites out to sea, carrying a fishing line. (There is no information available as to whether this fisherman invented the technique independently, or knew about primitive fishing-kites and simply adapted the idea to English conditions.) And in the U.S., in more recent years, fishing off shore by means of a kite has become quite popular (see below, p. 187). The technique enables one to fish beyond the breakers on an open shore-line.[1]

POLYNESIA

Kite-flying seems to have developed in Polynesia some time after the earliest days of that civilization. According to Nora Chadwick,[2] kites are not associated with the matriarchal volcano-gods of the early Polynesian religions, but became a highly important part of the later cults of Rongo, Tane, Rehua, etc., and were intimately associated with both the popular demi-god Maui and the Tawhaki hero-family from whose line chiefs so often claimed descent. It was mainly in North, East-central, and Southern Polynesia that kite-flying developed. It was of some importance also in New Zealand, but was relatively unknown in other parts of Western Polynesia.

The kite was thought of as a means of making contact with the gods and the heavens. There are many stories in which celestial communication takes place in this way. Kite-flying formed a particular part of the general rituals of the sky-cult. In their most highly developed symbolic role kites appear to have represented the external souls of gods, heroes, and men. As the gods were frequently represented by birds, the transition to the kite – often bird-shaped and called by a word meaning 'bird' – was easily made. The gods, that is, were represented on occasions not only as living birds, but also as artificial birds: as kites.

Except in the case of children's kites, flown purely for amusement, only chiefs or men of some standing were normally permitted to take control of them. But although only males flew the kites, the latter might themselves be of either sex. In some stories kites, playing the roles of gods and goddesses, actually mate and produce offspring.

[1] The anthropological and geographical details concerning kite-fishing in the Pacific may be found in three excellent published sources (see bibliography under Anell, Balfour, and Plischke).

[2] Chadwick, N. K., 'The Kite: a Study in Polynesian Tradition', *Journal of the Royal Anthropological Institute of Great Britain and Ireland*, Vol. 61, 1931, pp. 455–91.

Tawhaki is said to have mounted to heaven in the form of a kite (singing a kite-song on the way), and the god Tane is represented in similar fashion, though he is picturesquely said to be somewhat hindered in his upward flight by catching his long kite-tail in the trees.

There is a constant two-way symbolic association of kites and gods. On the one hand, the gods are represented as kites, while on the other, kite-competitions in Hawaiian stories are described as struggles between the gods and the elements. The gods themselves, in their celestial games, are said to have indulged in kite-competi-

Fig. 24. Maori bird-kites

tions, and there is reason to believe that the chiefs ritually emulated the gods in this respect.[1]

The intimate relationship between the kite and the gods brings about the curious tradition that Rehua, the god of highest heaven and of health, is to be thought of not only as a sacred bird, but also as the kite-'ancestor', from whom all other kites are descended.

Another, rather more commonplace, Polynesian version of the origin of the kite is quoted by W. W. Gill:

[1] For an exciting account of kite-god experiences, see Westervelt, W. D., *Legends of Ma-ui, a Demi God*, Honolulu, 1910, pp. 114–18.

Tane in the shades once challenged Rongo to a game of kite-flying. But the issue of this trial of skill was the utter discomfiture of Tane by his elder brother Rongo, who had secretly provided himself with an enormous amount of string. From this first kite-flying mortals have acquired the agreeable pastime, the condition of each game being that the first kite that mounts the sky should be sacred to, and should bear the name of, Rongo, the great patron of the art. The names of all *subsequent* kites were indifferent.[1]

(Ever since then Rongo has presided over peace and war, over the dead, and over kite-flying.)

The divine origin and significance of Polynesian kites is reflected by their use in early Polynesian society. Chiefs were associated with special forms of kite, so that a kind of kite-heraldry was established and kites became an important component in certain rituals. They were, for instance, appealed to for matters of divination. The following story is quoted from Elsdon Best:

> Some four hundred years ago there was trouble at Turanga over the death of two boys named Tara-ki-uta and Tara-ki-tai, who had been slain by a chief named Rakai-hikuroa. The mother of the missing lads, being unable to trace them, or detect the cause of their death, placed the matter in the hands of priestly experts. Those experts constructed two *taratahi* kites, which were named after the missing lads, and flown with appropriate ceremonial as an act of divination, in order to discover the person who had been responsible for the disappearance of the boys. Tradition states that both kites persistently hovered over Te Upoko o Taraia, the fortified village of Rakai-hikuroa, situated on a hill near Repo-ngaere Lake, hence a force at once marched to attack that place. The fight ended in the discomfiture of the guilty chief, whose son Tupurupuru was slain.[2]

As this story indicates, the kite was an important piece of equipment for the Polynesian *tohunga* (priestly adept). It was not only a means of divination, but might also function as a demon-queller, especially when an important voyage was to be undertaken. (This latter use is very reminiscent of Marco Polo's story about Chinese kites.)

Since the kite was a means of communication with the heavens, high-flying was commonly practised, using immense lengths of fibre twine. There is a story of one Polynesian hero who was said to have been able to fly his kite from under the water. Nora Chadwick suggests that this originates from the observation of large kites

---

[1] Gill, W. W., *Myths and Songs from the South Pacific*, London, 1876, p. 123.
[2] Best, E., *Games and Pastimes of the Maori*, Wellington, 1925, p. 76.

flown so high as to be visible above the horizon when the flier himself was out of sight. This explanation is not impossible, given the immense size which some Polynesian kites seem to have attained. High-flying competitions among the elders are described by W. W. Gill:

> In times of peace this was the great delight of aged men. Kites were usually five feet in length, covered with native cloth, on which were the devices appropriate to their tribe–a sort of heraldry. The tail was twenty fathoms in length, ornamented with a bunch of feathers and abundance of sere *ti* leaves. Parties were got up of not less than ten kite-flyers; the point of honour being that the kite should fly high, and be lost to view in the clouds. Songs made for the occasion were chanted meantime. It was no uncommon event for them to sleep on the mountain, after well securing the kites to the trees. Of course the upshot of all this would be a grand feast, in which the victor got the biggest share. So serious was this employment that each kite bore its own name, and tears of joy were shed by these grey-bearded children as they witnessed the successful flight. When desirous at length of putting an end to their sport, if the wind were too strong to allow the string to be pulled in, it was customary to fill a little basket with mountain fern or grass, and whirl it along the string. The strong trade winds would speedily convey this 'messenger' to the kite, which then slowly descended to earth.[1]

Kites were, however, also used for other than ceremonial and quasi-ceremonial purposes. In some parts of Polynesia, especially Hawaii, they were put to a variety of practical uses, such as aids to meteorology (and hence to navigation), weapons of war, and a means of claiming land. The last purpose was achieved by releasing a kite and laying claim to the area in which it fell. The gods, not man, had decided.

In Maori warfare the kite was used as a bringer of good fortune and as a means of terrifying the enemy. Elsdon Best writes:

> A kite was made of the culms of the *toetoe whatu manu*, a sedge, and was made so as to measure *pae tahi* (a fathom) from wing to wing. It was made by the chief *tohunga* . . . and certain restrictions prevailed during its manufacture. No member of the force was allowed to partake of food during that time, for the task pertained to the department of Tu, whose *tapu* affected every act of a war party, and the object of flying it was to gain the aid of Tu (god of war). The string used to fly this kite was not the usual kite cord but merely strips of undressed flax tied together, inasmuch as the kite was not recovered, but liberated. The kite was set up and flown by the *tohunga* who was careful to slack out the line with his right hand,

[1] Gill, W. W., *From Darkness to Light in Polynesia*, London, 1894, pp. 39-40.

Fig. 26. Kite of plaited leaves, from the Carolines

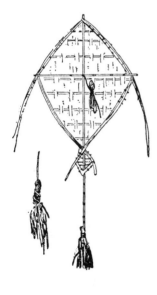

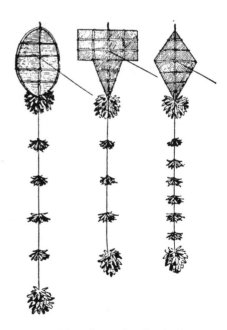

Fig. 25. **Kite from the Banks Group**

Fig. 27. Kites from the Cook Group

for that is the *tapu* side of man. Were he so forgetful as to do so with his left hand, the act would be an omen of defeat for his party.

Should the kite chance to fly in a lopsided manner it was accepted as a presage of defeat for the party should it deliver an attack. If it ascended in an upright and orthodox position that fact was accepted as an omen of success. While the kite was ascending, the *tohunga* recited the kite flying charm termed a *turu*. After the recital of the charm the warriors were at liberty to partake of food and so leave the *tohunga* at his task. The next act of the latter was to send a *karere* (messenger) up

Fig. 28.
Small kite for children
(Flies point upwards)

the cord to the kite. He formed a ring of *toetoe* leaves round the line, weaving it so that it was about 4 in. in diameter, so allowing plenty of space for the line. This ring was carried up the cord by the wind, and when it so arrived, the operator released the string and liberated the kite. This kite was always flown on the windward side of the *pa*, the object being to liberate it from such a point that, when drifting free, the cord thereof would be trailed across the *pa* of the enemy. Should any of the enemy chance to take hold of the trailing cord, which was more deadly than a 'live' wire, the act was an excellent omen for the attacking force, for it practically ensured the success of an attack on the fort; for that cord possessed magic properties with which it had been endowed by the incantations of the *tohunga*. When that cord was touched by one of the enemy it meant that their forces would be so affected by the magic rite that victory would assuredly follow an attack on them.[1]

The Polynesian kites, though consistently associated with birds, were not always of bird shape. There were many other types of figure-kite, representing men, turtles, men-of-war, etc. Some other configurations are shown in Figs. 25-27. The kites were made of wood, rushes, bark, and *tapa* (native cloth). Sometimes they were painted or adorned with feathers and shells, the latter producing a frightening rattle when the kite was in flight. (Shells were also sometimes placed inside hollow figure-heads on the kites, these being adorned at times with dog's hair.) In addition, one form of large kite, the *manu whara*, was armed with projecting spikes which made it, as it swooped about like a live hawk, a terrifying and lethal object to launch.

Some of the Polynesian kites may have been large enough to act as man-lifters. They certainly required whole teams of men to fly them. There is at least one Maori story of the use of the kite to raise a man:

> It appears that Nuku was trying to take a fortified village known as Maunga-rake, which, however, defied all his efforts at first. He then conceived the brilliant idea of lowering a man from an adjacent cliff or hillside by means of a kite, under cover of night, so that he might open up the gateway of the *pa* to admit the besiegers; the garrison keeping no watch apparently. The story goes:–'He built a huge *raupo* kite, something in the shape of a bird with great extended wings, and during the darkness of night he fastened one of his men to this kite and floated him over the cliff by means of a cord into the *pa* below. The man quietly opened up the entrance, and, when all was ready, at a given signal, Nuku lowered his men, four and five together, by means of a forest vine, and before morning the *pa* was taken.'[2]

According to Best, very large kites were sometimes launched from a sloping scaffolding which recalls the launching trestles of the Japanese *wan-wan*. (It is interesting to note that due to the difficulty of controlling and landing kites of such dimensions, the Maoris developed the techniques of under-running the line, and of flying with twin lines. See below, p. 190.) The great Maori birds have, unfortunately, been unknown, except in museums, for at least a century.

All the Polynesian kites so far discussed were, as I have said, flown by men.

[1] Best, *op. cit.*, pp. 70–71.
[2] *Ibid.*, p. 79.

Kites of lesser size and cruder construction were flown by children as a pastime. Fig. 28 represents one such kite. Kite-flying is still popular among the children of the Pacific but, there as elsewhere, the indigenous kites have often disappeared or been modified out of recognition due to contact with other cultures and other technologies. In Hawaii, for instance, kite-flying has been influenced by the large numbers of children of oriental birth. In the spring there is, as in China, a special 'kite-day' on which competitions are held.

As the above account may serve to indicate, the kite was an almost essential part of Polynesian life and thought. It probably played a more important role in Polynesia than it has ever done in any other civilization, serving, as it did, as religious symbol, aid to fishing, weapon of war, object of divination, and instrument of meteorology. Its omnipresence is reflected in its use as a simile in a number of proverbs. Colenso quotes a pleasing one used by a lover, expressive of his impatience at not being able to get away to see the beloved: *He manuaute e taea te whakahoro* ('a kite of aute-bark may be made to fly fast . . .').

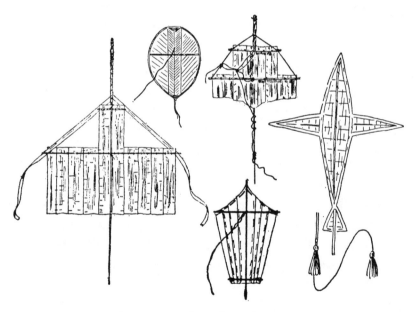

Fig. 29. More kites from the Pacific

4 | Early European Kites

It has been suggested that some form of kite was known among the ancients, but the evidence is very scanty. The wooden dove invented by Archytas of Tarentum about 400 B.C. has, together with its Chinese contemporaries devised by Mo Ti and Kungshu Phan, sometimes been taken to be a kite.[1] A theory has been advanced that Archytas had some contact with the east and that his dove was in fact the first importation of the Chinese invention. I know of no evidence to support this idea, though the date and manner of the first influence of eastern kites on the west are far from certain.

In early times there were no very clear distinctions between the various kinds of flying-machines, real or imaginary, which were all thought of as wonders and were usually described in very imprecise language. It may be that Archytas' dove was what we would call a kite today, but if it was, it failed to encourage others to try their hand at the art.[2] Nothing in classical literature can be taken with any certainty as an allusion to kites. Hodgson,[3] among others, was not prepared entirely to dismiss the possibility, but the case is far from convincing. Perhaps the most interesting evidence which suggested to earlier historians that kites were used by the ancients is a scene depicted on a vase (No. 3151) in the National Museum in Naples.[4] A female figure is holding a line at the end of which is a triangular-shaped

---

[1] This is not attested before the second century A.D. See Aulus Gellius, *Noctium atticarum libri xx*, X, 12, 8.

[2] Laufer, B., *The Prehistory of Aviation,* Chicago, 1928, p. 37.

[3] Hodgson, J. E., *The History of Aeronautics in Great Britain,* Oxford, 1924, p. 368.

[4] The suggestion that the object on the end of the string might be a kite was first made in the *Archäologische Zeitung,* Vol. 25, 1867, pp. 125–6. The vase is Greek, fourth century B.C.

object which for a hundred years some people thought to be a kite (Fig. 30). Plischke[1] suggested that, because of the slackness of the string, the scene might rather represent a game still played by Thessalonian children, in which a piece of paper is allowed to blow in the wind at the end of a cord. This differs, of course, from kite-flying in that no lift is produced. Eventually the mystery was solved when Mr Gibbs-Smith sought expert advice on the illustration and received an answer which now seems obvious, though everyone had been baffled for a century. The object is a spinning bobbin. The evidence for kites in ancient Europe is now virtually non-existent. Until further information comes to hand we may assume that, with the possible exception of some individuals who may have come across kites due to the trading contacts, the Greeks and Romans knew nothing of them.

Fig. 30. Figure on a 4th-century B.C. Greek vase in Naples. Once thought to be a kite, but actually a spinning bobbin

How, then, did kites originate in Europe? Attempts have been made to trace their source through the near east or from the far east, via the Portuguese, English, and Dutch trade routes. The familiar modern plane-surface kite can undoubtedly be traced back to such sources, but to these must be added a further and quite different source dating back to classical times, the exact nature of which has only recently been elucidated.

The story of European kites may be said to begin with an unlikely object, the spectacular *draco,* or windsock banner, which was a familiar sight in Europe during the later days of the Roman Empire, and which played a rather curious role in the early history of unmanned flight. It consisted of a carved open-mouthed head, of

[1] Plischke, H., 'Alter und Herkunft des Europäischen Flächendrachens', *Nachrichten von der Gesellschaft der Wissenschaften zu Göttingen,* Phil.-Hist. Kl., N.F., Fachgr. 2, Vol. 2, No. 1, 1936, pp. 1–18.

dragon-like appearance, attached to the top of a pole. Behind the head was fixed a tube of cloth which billowed out in the wind when the standard was held aloft by the *draconarius*. This standard appears to have been used in the first place to terrify the enemy and to inspire courage in the troops of the cohort, but it may also have been used for signalling, and it could have served to help archers to judge the strength of the wind. It was certainly used for ceremonial purposes.[1]

The origin of the *draco* is obscure, but it seems to have arisen somewhere in central Asia, where it continued in use at least until the Middle Ages. Whether it was ever used in China is uncertain, but what may have been a Chinese windsock standard is depicted on a beautifully decorated dish, of the K'ang-hsi period (1662-1722), in the Fitzwilliam Museum (Plate 17). The banner looks three-dimensional and seems to billow out from a ring attached to the pole,[2] but the appearance may be deceptive, and may be attributable to the modelling of the thick layers of under-glaze blue. Similar scenes are found on many Chinese plates and dishes from the period, and, in every other example that I have seen, the banner, although given something of the same billowing appearance, is unmistakably flat. While it is therefore possible that windsock standards were known, if not common, in seventeenth- and eighteenth-century China, the date of this dish is much too late to be used as evidence of Chinese origins of the *draco*. There is, however, no doubt that more than a thousand years earlier the standard was well known to the Scythians, Persians, and Dacians, among others.[3] At some time around the third century A.D. this form of standard was adopted by the Romans. While at first it appears to have been used only by auxiliaries, it later became the regular standard of a cohort, being second in importance to the *aquila* of the legion.[4] Although it continued to be found in Europe after the fall of Rome, it was most commonly associated with the eastern 'barbarians'.

[1] Renel, C., *Cultes militaires de Rome: les enseignes,* Paris, 1903, pp. 206-11.

[2] In a private communication, dated January 1, 1969, Dr Joseph Needham expresses his agreement with my interpretation of the standard.

[3] *E.g.,* Arrian, *Tactics,* 35. 2ff; Lucian, *How to Write History,* 29. For further references see the article on the *draco* in *Paulys Realencyclopädie der Classischen Altertumswissenschaft,* ed. G. Wissowa, Stuttgart, 1893, etc.

[4] Vegetius, II. 13 (14): *primum signum totius legionis est aquila: quam Aquilifer portat. Dracones etiam per singulas cohortes a Draconariis feruntur ad proelium.*

Fig. 31. Dacian windsock standard
on the Trajan column,
early first century A.D.

Fig. 32. The windsock standard
extended by the breeze

The dragon standards were often made to look very realistic, with the result that some reports seem to attribute animal life to them. Lucian is scornful of one such gullible commentator:

> . . . he has seen everything so keenly that he said that the serpents of the Parthians (this is a banner they use to indicate number—a serpent precedes, I think, a thousand men), he said that they were alive and of enormous size; that they are born in Persia a little way beyond Iberia; that they are bound to long poles and, raised on high, create terror while the Parthians are coming on from a distance; that in the encounter itself at close quarters they are freed and sent against the enemy; that in fact they had swallowed many of our men in this way and coiled themselves around others and suffocated and crushed them . . .[1]

The dragons on the Trajan column, which are shown as forming a part of the accoutrement of the defeated Dacians, certainly look real enough (Fig. 31), while Ammianus Marcellinus provides a vivid description of the lifelike ceremonial *dracones* which surrounded the emperor:

> And behind the manifold others that preceded him he was surrounded by dragons, woven out of purple thread and bound to the golden and jewelled tops of spears, with

[1] *How to Write History,* 29. (Loeb, vol. 6, pp. 42, 43.)

wide mouths open to the breeze and hence hissing as if roused by anger, and leaving their tails winding in the wind.[1]

The continuity of the *draco* can be traced through its appearance in the *Psalterium*

Figs. 33, 34. Windsock standards from the Bayeux Tapestry

aureum (Plate 18), in the Bayeux Tapestry (Figs. 33, 34), and in the *Chanson de Roland*, where it is attributed to the pagans, in contrast to the flat banner of the Christians.

At some time during the early Middle Ages there arose the practice of enhancing the appearance of the dragon by placing a lighted torch in its mouth, thus causing it to emit fire and smoke, as may be seen in Plate 18. It is possible that the red dragon used to such good effect by Merlin was an imaginative recreation of the fire-breathing standard:

> . . . then Merlin turned the dragon in his hand and it shot forth flames of fire from its mouth so that the air was quite reddened . . .[2]

The first definitive written evidence of the use of such fire in the dragons is a well-

---

[1] *Rerum gestarum libri qui supersunt,* XVI. 10.7. (Loeb vol. 1, pp. 244, 245.)

[2] *Lestoire de Merlin,* ed. H. O. Sommer, Washington, 1908, p. 225: *lors sen tourne merlins le dragon en sa main qui ietoit brandons de feu parmi la goule que li airs en deuint tous vermaus . . .*

known passage in Długosz's *Historia polonica,* describing the battle of Wahlstatt, near Lignica, in April, 1241:

> Among other standards there was, in the Tartar army, an immense banner on which a sign like an X was to be seen. And at the top of the enemy banner was the representation of a hideous, jet-black head with a bearded chin. During the pursuit on the slopes, when the Tartars had withdrawn to the distance of a *stadium,* the standard-bearer began with all his strength to shake the head which was on top of a spear, and from it there poured forth vile-smelling steam, smoke, and fumes, which engulfed the whole Polish army. Because of the horrible and intolerable fumes, the Polish warriors, nearly unconscious and half dead, were weak and unable to fight. [1]

The later development of the fire-breathing *draco,* as I shall point out, grows rather confused, the confusion arising from errors of interpretation by both mediaeval and modern writers on the subject.

In the late nineteenth century it was noticed that among the most spectacular inventions included in mediaeval technological treatises was something superficially similar to a kite, but having a body in the shape of an elongated dragon. The main part of the body was usually drawn in a manner suggesting suppleness, while instructions for building it, which sometimes accompanied the illustrations, indicated that is was made of wood, parchment, and cloth. As such kites were shown flying from the ends of cords, it was apparent that a form of sustentation was implied, at least in theory. Occasionally wings were drawn, though they were sometimes very small, and five of the creatures are shown emitting fire and smoke. Until recently it has been assumed that these were primitive hot-air balloons, the fire and smoke pointing to the use inside the dragon's mouth of a slow-burning match which warmed the air within the fabric sufficiently to produce sustentation.

When one examines the published work concerning these so-called 'semi-kites', it becomes apparent that the interpretation both of their form and of their method of flight has been supported by only two passages of contemporary text, bolstered by a substantial amount of supposition. The textual evidence is found on ff. 104[v] and 105[r] of Conrad Kyeser's *Bellifortis* (1405).[2] On the latter page Kyeser's miniaturist has drawn a dragon-kite which has become very familiar to aeronautical historians (Plate 19). This illustration is intended to accompany a ten-line text written, like

---

[1] Długosz, J., *Historiae polonicae libri xii,* Lipsiae, 1711-12, col. 679.
[2] Göttingen, Niedersächsische Staats- und Universitätsbibliothek, codex philos. 63.

most of *Bellifortis,* in bad Latin hexameters. The text describes the structure and mode of flight: 'This flying dragon may be made with parchment for the head, the middle of linen, but the tail of silk, the colours various. At the end of the head let a triple harness [bridle] be attached to the wood, moved by the middle of the flail [-shaped reel]. Let the head be raised into the wind, and when it has been lifted two men may hold the head while a third carries the reel. It follows him while he rides [or, 'he follows it as he rides']. The movement of the line causes the flight to vary up and down, to right and left. Let the head be coloured red and made to look real, the middle should be of moon-silver colour, the end of several colours.' The diagram to the right of Plate 19 shows the method of attaching the bridle.

On the previous page (104ᵛ) there occurs a passage, headed *Ignis pro Tygace uolante,* which gives details of a recipe for making fire-producing materials. It has been assumed that the fire was intended for the *draco,* and, therefore, that the *draco* and the *tygax* were identical. This explanation has gained currency largely due to the work of Feldhaus and Romocki.[1]

The supposition that the two texts were meant to accompany one another has led, in the first place, to the idea that the *draco* on f. 105ʳ consisted of a hollow tube into which a dish containing the fire could be introduced, and in the second place to the development of an extensive theory to account for the origin of this technologically sophisticated object.

It was not unnatural that, given the passage containing the fire-producing recipe in Kyeser, commentators should have believed that his *draco,* though flying free on a cord rather than held on a rigid pole, carried fire in the same way as did the old dragon standards. Someone had noticed that the hot air produced buoyancy in the dragon's tail, and had hit upon the idea of allowing the whole thing to rise on the end of a string. While the theory is attractive at first sight, it does not withstand close scrutiny. In the first place, it is plainly impossible that, using the materials available at the time, dragons could have been made light enough to rise when filled with hot air. This objection loses some force, of course, if we treat the semi-kite, like many other objects drawn in manuscripts of the Kyeser type, as imaginary.

---

[1] Feldhaus, F. M., *Die Technik der Vorzeit,* Leipzig und Berlin, 1914, cols. 650-9; von Romocki, S. J., *Geschichte der Explosivstoffe,* vol. 1, Berlin, 1895, pp. 160-2.

As I go on to discuss below, it is nevertheless possible to interpret the *draco,* in an entirely different sense, as a reasonably accurate representation of reality.

The second and more serious objection concerns the relationship of the passages on ff. 104^v and 105^r of codex philos. 63. In a little-known article published in 1940, F. Denk questioned the relevance of the one to the other, suggesting that the word *tygax* might refer rather to a firearm illustrated on the same page.[1] The problem is the more acute in that *tygax* appears to be a nonce word of unknown meaning. Denk seems to have failed, however, to notice that the *tygax* page is the last in an interpolated passage not written by Kyeser himself, but based on the *Liber ignium* of Marcus Graecus.[2] The consequences of this are twofold: first, the ten-line text on f. 105^r is the only evidence of Kyeser's own intention regarding the *draco,* and, second, the interpolated passage, if it does indeed refer to the *draco,* represents someone else's interpretation of its nature and function.

The rest of Kyeser's short text, taken alone, bears no implication of three-dimensionality. Furthermore, the *draco* is very similar to a kite described some twenty-five years later in Vienna codex 3064, one of many mediaeval 'fireworks-books' (Plate 21).[3] The description in this case is lengthy and detailed, and the object is undoubtedly a kite of the plane-surface type. The kite in the 'fireworks-book' was certainly built and flown, the description being written in a manner which indicates very clearly that the writer was a practised kite-flier. The Kyeser drawing could, without difficulty, be interpreted as a representation of a kite similar in all important respects to that in Vienna codex 3064. Both the scanty details of its construction and the comments on its mode of flight are consistent with the latter text. Such an interpretation would therefore retrieve the *draco* from the realm of fantasy. I think it highly likely that Kyeser meant to depict a real plane-surface kite which could be built and flown, and that the *tygax* page, if it refers to the drawing, was meant to provide a fire-producing recipe for a three-dimensional kite of an imaginary kind, based on a misinterpretation of the *draco* by the writer of the interpolation.

[1] Denk, F., 'Zwei mittelalterliche Dokumente zur Fluggeschichte und ihre Deutung,' *Sitzungsberichte der Physikalischmedizinischen Sozietät in Erlangen,* vol. 71, 1939, pp. 353-68. (Published Erlangen, 1940.)

[2] Quarg, G., 'Der BELLIFORTIS von Conrad Kyeser aus Eichstätt, 1405,' *Technikgeschichte,* vol. 32, no. 4, 1965, pp. 318-20.

[3] See below, pp. 70-72.

A possible source of confusion of windsocks and plane-surface kites is to be found in the description of the kite in Vienna codex 3064 (Plate 21). In the notes for its construction the writer says that it would be best to 'cut it open down the middle of the back for two or three ells, starting from the head, and then insert and sew in a piece of silk cloth one and a half spans wide, more or less, and pointed at both ends, following the shape of the body'. He points out that the effect of this insertion is to create a sail-like fulness which, he claims, both improves the flight and makes the kite appear to have a three-dimensional body or back. It may be that the use of such wind-filled pockets led to confusion, in the minds of some early interpreters of Kyeser, about the structure of the *draco*. Alternatively the pocket may, of course, have been an attempt to produce a simple practical realisation of the probably imaginary windsock-kite.

The detailed arguments about the many variant copies of Kyeser's kite are set out in my book *The Dream of Flight*.[1] For the present purposes the dragon may be compared with two other mediaeval kites, the first of which is probably plane-surface, and the second of which is undoubtedly so. The dragon sketched in Walter de Milemete's *De nobilitatibus* (1326/27) is the earliest known illustration of a European kite (Fig. 35). Since, unfortunately, it occurs in a part of the manuscript which is only sketched in, ready for later completion by the illuminator, the construction of the kite is unclear. Some features of it suggest that it could have been three-dimensional (that is, that its body was a windsock). The loop in the tail, which may represent a knot, is one such feature. A knot might have been intended to close the rear orifice and so retain the wind, but this, as with so many other details from mediaeval manuscripts, may represent convention or supposition rather than fact. Dragons were commonly drawn with knotted tails. A second feature of interest is the provision of wings. These, though drawn very small, may in reality have been large enough to provide the necessary sustentation for a windsock.

Whatever the origin of the pennon shaped kites seen in the fourteenth- and fifteenth-century manuscripts, their physical existence in mediaeval Europe is beyond question. The text which accompanies Plate 21 was undoubtedly written by someone with first-hand knowledge of such things. The description of the construction and of the mode of manipulation, though repetitive, crude in style,

[1] London, 1972, pp. 38-43.

Fig. 35. Winged plane-surface kite in Walter de Milemete's *De nobilitatibus,* Oxford, Christ Church, MS 92, ff. 77ᵛ-78ʳ, 1326/7.

and occasionally obscure, is entirely factual and is an accurate reflection of physical reality. Although nothing is known of the author, the manuscript has been dated *ca.* 1430:

> How you can make an artificial kite and how to handle it so that it hovers in the air and moves as if it were alive.
>
> Take a piece of silk cloth of red, green, or other colour; alternatively the cloth may be of mixed colours, like a snake if you wish. The red colour, however, stands out much the best when it is seen in the air, and especially against the sun, as though it were something fiery. Or again you may take or prepare gilt cloth, so that it is very bright and fiery. But in any case let it be of very lightweight cloth. And have the kite cut out of the cloth and shaped according to the design of the figure drawn opposite, and so constructed that it have a head made of a sheet of parchment which is fine but nevertheless strong enough to keep the face stiff. And

the head should be of the same size as a broad sheet of parchment; the total length of the body behind the head, together with the tail, should be eleven ells; and the body at the sheet which forms the head should be as wide as the head; and in the middle, at the sides, there should be placed something billowing or winglike, so that it have a dragonlike appearance. It is especially advisable, if the kite is to be exactly right, to make an incision two or three ells in lengths from the head down the middle of the back, and to sew into the middle of it a piece of silk cloth a span and a half wide, more or less, and pointed at both ends like the [lower end of the] kite itself. Then, if the wind strikes it, it fills out in the manner of a sail and flies up more lightly into the wind and takes on the shape of a raised body or back, which makes it much better and more lifelike, as you find in the figure given here. [These and other details are not, in fact, shown in the illustration.] Nevertheless, if you do not make this insertion it will be quite adequate. And when the body has been made in this way, have the head painted with a striking dragonlike face on the parchment sheet, which should be kept quite bright and shiny by the use of light colours. And then sew the head on to the body and at each corner of the parchment make two or three little loops formed of three or four strands of thread, and let both sides of the head-sheet, where the loops are attached, be strengthened with little patches of parchment, so that the loops will cut through it the less. And then obtain small batons which have been cut and split from good new tough fir sticks, so as to be one finger broad and half as thick as a rye-stalk [?]. Place the batons crosswise over one another on the head and fix them in the loops so that in the middle they are bowed out from the face to a distance of two fingers' breadth; and at the middle of the cross they may be bound with another loop as a protection against the wind, as you find drawn in the picture. If the wind is very strong, and you think the head may bend too much and the batons break, you may place another baton outside the kite, over the head—also [? held by] a loop—and across all this one [baton], or as many as may be needed, over the skull, from the middle of the head where it meets the back, as far up as to the forehead. If the wind is still stronger you may make this baton thicker. Or if it is very strong indeed you may place a stick of a finger's breadth over the skull, from the back to the fore-head, as stated before. After that you should make three loops between the eyes, from the forehead down to the nose, as is shown here. And push the string, from which you wish to fly the kite, through one or the other of them and tie it to the third, that is, the lowest, as you also find drawn. However, if the wind is too strong, put the string through the topmost and wind it around the middle one. If the wind is yet stronger, wind it on to the top one alone. If it is still too strong, however, place the thick stick over its head, as described before, and tie the string to the stick at the top of the forehead and let it fly as it will. If you now wish to make it fly, go where you have wind and hold it upright so that the wind strikes it in the face and in the body, and when the wind blows fairly strongly lift it right up and let it go with the string; thus it will rise, and you must all the while let it out carefully. If the wind is rather weak, walk against the wind so that the kite is opposed to it and in this way you will force it with the wind as high as you wish. When it has reached the height of one or two towers, and is well up in the air, you may guide it where you wish, using these methods of control, as long as the ground on which you are walking is sufficiently even: If you want to make it move into the wind, pull it gently and [then] let it have free rein, and it will go further and higher. If you want it to fly away with the wind [?], you must walk towards it and gently release it and it will move away. And it is good to ease it out very slowly, almost as if it were stationary, and then it will move in a soaring manner wherever you wish, and will not seem to be moving back. And then if it has flown over a town or a hill you can pull it back or across wherever you wish. But you should take note whether the wind is too weak. If the kite hangs its head or bends towards itself you must run quickly against the wind so that the wind blows against it and it rights itself. But when it raises its head you may direct it where you wish, using the techniques which have been described. When you want to bring it down again, walk some distance back so that when it has almost come down, in case the wind is then almost still, it will not fall to the ground before you have brought it right in or it may be caught in a tree or bush. If people threaten to approach and pester you to see it when it is being brought down, get your assistant to hold the string as if it were he who were bringing it down and take the string under your elbow and hold it in the other hand so that in case it breaks under your elbow you still have it in your hand, and walk towards it until it comes to the ground and there take the batons out and fold the head together and wrap the body around it and hide it. It is also advisable, when you are controlling it with the string, that you should have an assistant with you who may walk directly under the kite, wherever it moves, so that if the string should break he may see where the kite comes to earth, so that it may not be lost. When the kite comes down it falls immediately under where it is flying; it does not fall more than one or two pike-lengths away, and so is not lost by that assistant. And it is good to have the assistant there so that many people may imagine that it is he who is controlling the kite, and thus he who is controlling it attracts less attention. If you want the kite to move down at particular places as if it were diving at the earth or at people, that also you may perform by skilful handling. Note too that with some care you can arrange that four or six smaller and larger kites fly together, as if the young ones were flying with the old one; and you can arrange that they fly one above the other, and are nevertheless controlled by a single string or line. Note also that following the preceding directions you may make the kite very big indeed, so as to create great astonishment.[1]

---

[1] Vienna, Österreichische Nationalbibliothek, codex 3064, ff. 4^{v}–7^{r}.

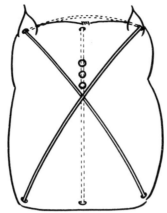

Fig. 36. Structure of the head of the pennon kite
in Vienna codex 3064.
The optional sticks are shown dotted

Fig. 37. Insertion of extra fulness for the body of
the pennon kite

The details of the structure are redrawn in Fig. 36, and the additional fulness for the
body is shown in Fig. 37. A reproduction of the kite, which flies well, is shown in
Plate 22. The head (18 in. × 24 in.) is of parchment, the body and tail of light
cotton. The extra piece of cloth has been inserted in the back, and an attempt has
been made to follow the instructions about the 'billowing and winglike' projections, which the writer suggests adding to the body to make it more lifelike. While
it is plain that no rigid, aerodynamically supporting surfaces are intended, ornamental projections of the kind described may have been the origin of the probably
imaginary wings found on so many of the copies of the Kyeser *draco*. The writer
seems to have had in mind appendages such as are shown behind the creature's
head in Plate 18.

The prescribed method of landing by pressing down the line and walking
towards the kite, now known as 'underrunning', was independently developed by

fliers of meteorological kites in the late nineteenth and early twentieth centuries. The method is especially useful for landing in a high wind (Plate 50).

The instructions regarding the three loops, or rings, for flying in varying wind strengths, are in conformity with the performance to be expected from kites of this type, though the method of attachment is much less satisfactory than the use of a bridle, as specified in Kyeser's text. None of the miniaturists who depicted Kyeser's *draco* fully understood the passage about the *tripla zona,* and the only one to have drawn it at all (see Plate 20c) showed it attached in an impossible way, but there is little doubt that what was intended was something like Fig. 38.

Fig. 38
Probable attachment of
the bridle to kites of
the Kyeser type

Apart from the Kyeser series, I know of only two other representations of mediaeval kites showing a general similarity to the one in Vienna codex 3064. These are the Milemete kite (1326/7) and a military standard in a Russian icon, also of the fourteenth century (Plate 24), which is probably a pennon kite of the same general configuration. The icon, from St Nicholas' Church in Nizhni-Novgorod, celebrates a battle between the Novgorodians and the invading Suzdalians, who remained in possession of the city during the thirteenth and fourteenth centuries. The shape of the kite, if it is indeed one, gives further support to the possibility that such kites were of eastern origin. It is also possible, as Duhem suggests,[1] that this banner bears some historical relationship to the fire-breathing *draco* standard used by the Mongols at Wahlstatt, as described by Długosz.

Nothing from the period can be found to compare with the text of Vienna codex 3064. No such description of a kite and its manipulation is, indeed, to be seen again before modern times, and no other unequivocal description of any sort appears before 1558. During this period of over a hundred years there appear, however, at least four other accounts, of a somewhat doubtful nature, which may refer to kite-flying. The first concerns the talented German mathematician and astronomer Johannes Müller von Königsberg, who was better known under his Latinised pseudonym Regiomontanus. He was born in Königsberg on June 6, 1436,

[1] Duhem, J., *Histoire des idées aéronautiques avant Montgolfier,* Paris, 1943, p. 195.

but left his home town in adolescence and travelled widely. In 1450 he was in Vienna, where he matriculated at the university. He was in Italy in 1461, and in Hungary in 1467. In the spring of 1471 he travelled to Nürnberg, where he settled, and with which city he is most commonly associated. There he stayed until July 28, 1475, when he left to visit Rome, where he was assassinated, at the age of 40, on July 6, 1476.[1] One of the many stories about Regiomontanus which circulated in the sixteenth, seventeenth, and eighteenth centuries tells of his having built, while at Nürnberg, both an artificial eagle and an iron fly. As far as I can determine, the earliest printed account, which seems to be the ultimate source of all the later ones, is to be found in Peter Ramus' *Scholarum mathematicarum libri unus et triginta.*:[2]

> . . . among the artful curiosities of Regiomontanus, one of the inventors of Nürnberg, was the device of allowing an iron fly, as if released from the hand of the artificer, to flutter around the guests, and then as if tired to return to the hand of its master; and of sending forth from the city, high into the air, an eagle to greet the Emperor on his arrival and accompany him to the city gates. After Nürnberg's revelation of the fly and of the eagle with geometrical wings, we cease to be amazed at Archytas' dove.

The 'emperor' mentioned here was, of course, the Holy Roman Emperor of the day, Frederick III (1452-93). Some later reports anachronistically name Maximilian I (1493-1519) or even Charles V (1519-58). Frederick did in fact visit Nürnberg in February and March 1473/4, when the flight of the eagle, if it is more than legend, must have taken place.

Although Regiomontanus' eagles might be interpreted as some form of free-flying automaton, I think it more likely that a kite is here being described, though in somewhat garbled fashion. A kite of the pennon shape, and perhaps equipped with wings, might readily be given the appearance of an eagle rather than of the by then traditional dragon. Partly owing to the misinterpretation of the so-called 'semi-kites', it has been assumed until recently that before the mid-sixteenth century kites were probably unknown or at least exceedingly rare in Europe. As the kite explanation did not offer itself, the story of Regiomontanus' eagle was usually taken to be fanciful. A quite searching investigation of the tradition,

---

[1] For biographical details of Regiomontanus, see E. Zinner, *Leben und Wirken des Joh. Müller von Königsberg genannt Regiomontanus,* rev. edn., Osnabrück, 1968.

[2] Basileae, 1569, lib. II, p. 65.

contained in a thesis by J. W. Baier and J. A. Bühel[1] which was presented at the university of Altdorf on January 29, 1707, concludes with the view that no such flight took place and that the story of the eagle was merely an exaggerated description of a large mechanical bird, with a hinged head, placed over the city gate. Zinner, who agrees with this interpretation, points out that the bird was first erected in 1541, for a visit by Charles V, an event which may help to explain the anachronism in those accounts which associate Charles V and Regiomontanus. In support of the many doubters of the truth of the story,[2] one must point to the very suspicious omission, from the meticulous and sober contemporary chronicles of the city of Nürnberg, of any mention of the flight.[3]

Indirect evidence to support the idea that the eagle may have existed in the form of a kite is found in a comparatively little known book, published in 1530, which describes a visit of Charles V to Munich in that year.[4] Charles, who was returning from coronation in Bologna, was met with great ceremony. Among the spectacles arranged in his honour was a flying dragon which welcomed him as he entered the city: 'When things had begun as indicated, His Majesty turned towards the town and his entry into it, and over the middle of his path there hung a flying dragon, most amazingly controlled, which hovered long in the air until the procession had passed.' Fortunately this dragon is represented in a large woodcut, also dated 1530, by Nikolaus Meldemann, which celebrates the same scene (Fig. 39). The dragon is there drawn with the same imaginative freedom that one finds in the copies of Kyeser's *draco,* and although no retaining line is shown, it seems probable that it was a kite. The anonymous writer's words, 'most amazingly controlled' (*vast wercklich zugericht),* suggest some kind of manipulation from the ground. Such a spectacle would certainly have been a practical possibility at the time, while the relative unfamiliarity of kites would easily explain the misrepresentation of the woodcut. The dragon is emitting fire and smoke, as do many of those in earlier illustrations, a detail which led von Bassermann-Jordan to make the assumption,

---

[1] *De aquila et musca ferrea, quæ mechanico artificio apud Noribergenses quondam volitasse feruntur,* Altorfiae, 1707.

[2] Duhem, J., *Histoire des idées aéronautiques avant Montgolfier,* Paris, 1943, pp. 128-30.

[3] Schedel, H., *Registrum hujus operis libri cronicarum . . .,* Nuremberge, 1493, f. cclv[r]; Zinner, *Leben und Wirken,* pp. 214-5.

[4] *Ain kurtze anzaygung und beschreybung . . .,* [Munich], 1530, [A4[r]]. The visit took place on June 10, 1530.

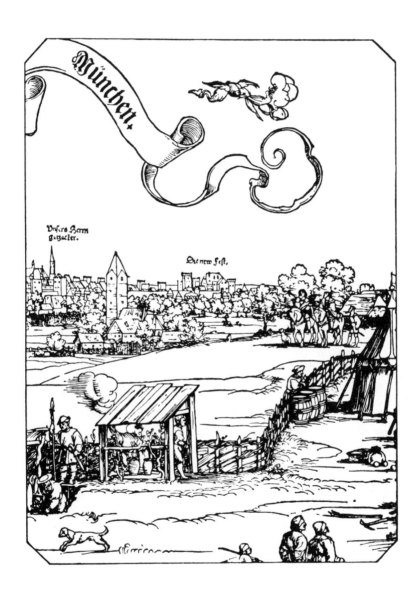

Fig. 39. Detail from a woodcut by Nicolas Meldemann, 1530,
showing a dragon (probably a kite) flying over Charles V
during his ceremonial entry into Munich.

reasonable enough when he was writing, that a hot-air 'semi-kite' was intended.[1] It is worth noting, however, that the description of the scene says nothing about fire, nor anything which might be taken to refer to rocket-propulsion, which suggests once again that the dragon was a kite. It seems likely that, together with the ceremonial use of the mechanical eagle in 1541, some conflation of this scene with the popular story of Regiomontanus' activities may have contributed to the confusion over the identity of the emperor.

The third possible allusion to a kite between 1430 and 1558 is contained in a story about Leonardo, who is said to have flown kites when on his way to Rome for the coronation of Pope Leo X in March 1512/13. The last, and slightest, of the four is a comment in Cardano's discussion of the famous wooden dove of Archytas. He speaks of the possibility of making 'a flying bird, but with a cord attached,' suggesting that he had once seen a kite, but it is clear that he was relatively unfamiliar with such things.

During the sixteenth and seventeenth centuries plane surface kites both of the dragon-shaped type and the better known pear and diamond shapes (see below) became increasingly common and it is during this period that an undoubted element of confusion arose with the older idea of a three-dimensional windsock. In the seventeenth century in particular there appear several fanciful descriptions of windsock kites which were probably attempts to translate into reality the imaginary three-dimensional shape suggested by the dragons. A particularly interesting example of this process of translation is to be found in Daniel Schwenter's *Deliciae physico-mathematicae*.[2] Although his ultimate source is a well-known chapter in della Porta describing what is certainly a plane-surface kite, Schwenter,

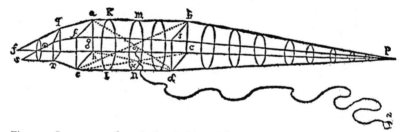

Fig. 40. Structure of a windsock kite. Schwenter, D., *Deliciæ physico-mathematicæ*, pt. 1, Nürnberg, 1636, p. 474

[1] von Bassermann-Jordan, E., *Alte Uhren und ihre Meister*, Leipzig, 1926, pp. 64–6.
[2] Schwenter, D., *Deliciæ physico-mathematicæ*, pt. 1, Nürnberg, 1636, pp. 472–5.

in recasting the description in the vernacular, distorts the plain meaning of the original text so as to provide, instead, details of a large windsock. Although no wings are shown in the diagram (Fig. 40) they are mentioned briefly in the text. Schwenter mentions the use of windsock kites to carry lamps and musical instruments, a subject which is taken up a number of times by Athanasius Kircher, whose illustrations of windsocks look, however, still further removed from reality (Fig. 41-43).

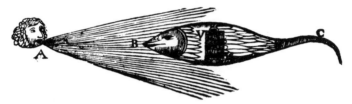

Fig. 41. Hypothetical windsock kite. Athanasius Kircher,
Musurgia universalis, Romae, 1650, vol. 2, p. 354

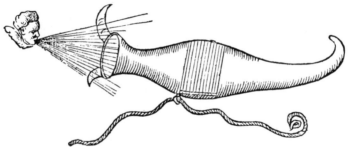

Fig. 42. A redrawing of Fig. 41. *Athanasii Kircheri e Soc. Jesu.*
phonurgia nova, Campidonae, 1673, p. 147

Some of the copies of Kyeser's *draco* seem to indicate that the *draco* standard, in the form of a windsock of frightening appearance and capable of carrying fire in the mouth, survived into early Renaissance times. The existence of free-flying windsocks, lifted by wings, seems much less likely, but the accounts in Schwenter and Kircher may perhaps reflect the reality of winged windsocks built and tested in the sixteenth and seventeenth centuries. As such objects would have been both difficult to construct and aerodynamically very inefficient, they were probably uncommon, to say the least, and in any case no more is heard of them after the seventeenth century.

A possible reason for the persistence of the dragon-shaped kites and standards

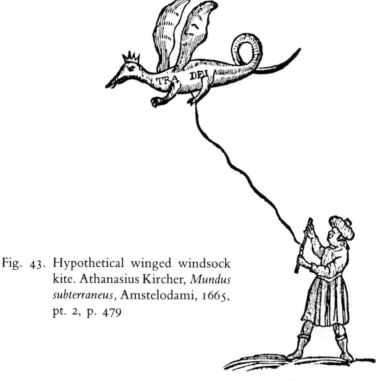

Fig. 43. Hypothetical winged windsock
kite. Athanasius Kircher, *Mundus
subterraneus,* Amstelodami, 1665,
pt. 2, p. 479

until the years of the New Science is to be found in their physical similarity to the
natural phenomenon called the *draco volans,* or 'fire drake', one of the more spectacular celestial events regularly noted by mediaeval and early Renaissance
meteorologists. The 'fire drake' was believed to consist of a dragon-like con-
glomeration of vapours in the lower air. William Fulke describes its formation:

> When a certen quantitie of *vapors* ar gathered on a heape, being very near compact,
> & as it wer hard tempered together this lompe of *vapors* assending to the region of
> cold, is forcibly beaten backe, whiche violence of mouing, is sufficient to kindle it,
> (although som men will haue it to be caused betwene ij. cloudes a whote & a cold)
> then the highest part, which was climming vpward, being by reason more subtil &
> thin, apeareth as the Dragons neck, smoking, for that it was lately in the repuls
> bowed or made crooked, to represent the dragons bely. The last part by the same
> repulse, turned vpward, maketh the tayle, both apearing smaller, for that it is
> farther of, & also, for that the cold bindeth it. This dragon thus being caused,
> flyeth along in the ayre, & somtime turneth to & fro, if it meat with a cold cloud
> to beat it back, to the great terror, of them that beholde it, of whom some called it

a fyre Drake, some saye it is the Deuill hym selfe, and so make report to other. More then sixtene yeares ago, on May daye, when many younge folke went abroade early in the mornyng, I remember, by sixe of the clocke in the forenoone, there was newes come to London, that the Deuill the same mornynge, was seene flyinge ouer the Temmes: afterward came worde, that he lyghted at Stratforde, and ther was taken and sett in the stockes, and that though he would fayne haue dissembled the matter, by turning hym selfe into the likenes of a man, yet was he knowen welinough by his clouen feet. I knowe some yet alyue, that went to see hym, & returning affirmed, that he was in deed seen flying in the ayre, but was not taken prysoner. I remember also that som wyshed he had been shoot at with gons, or shaftes as he flewe ouer the Temes. Thus do ignorant men iudge of these thynges that they knowe not, as for this Deuill, I suppose it was a flyinge Dragon, wherof we speake, very fearefull to loke vpon, as though he had life, because he moueth, where as he is nothing els but cloudes & smoke . . .[1]

Although I know of no texts which make an explicit connexion between the two kinds of *draco*, illustrations of the atmospheric 'flying dragon' (Fig. 44) are often very similar to the artificial creations in Plates 20c, 20d, etc., and it seems possible that the fire-breathing monster which some experimenters had hoped to make fly at the end of a cord was conceived as a crude man-made reproduction of the frightening 'meteor' with its satanic associations. Starting as a simple length of cloth on the end of a pole, the standard had, over the centuries, developed both increasingly lifelike and increasingly aerodynamic characteristics. The putative free-flying windsock with its sinuous movement and threatening mouth was potentially capable of transforming into reality the many old stories of manned flight. The potentiality must, however, have seemed too daring an idea for the courageous contemporary dabblers in aeronautical science, for no one suggested that the 'flying dragons' might be used to lift a man. The *dracones* were nevertheless of importance in shaping the history of flight. For two or three centuries they gave direct practical experience of the manipulation of wind forces, and they firmly established the kite in Europe. Had there been no *dracones,* virtually the only well-known aerodynamic objects in Europe before 1600 would have been passive and active windmills, whose potential importance for aeronautics was still less appreciated than was that of the kite.

Following the establishment of the New Science, 'observations' of such things as the meteoric *draco volans* grew less frequent. With the simultaneous growth of

[1] Fulke, W., *A Goodly Gallerye*, Londini, 1563, ff. 10ʳ-11ʳ.

Fig. 44. Conventional drawings of the meteorological phenomenon known as the 'flying dragon' may have influenced the
shape of the fifteenth and sixteenth century dragon-shaped
kites. From the *Kalendrier des Bergiers,* Paris, 1493.

popularity of the simpler pear and diamond kites, the old dragon shapes, both
plane-surface and three-dimensional, went entirely out of fashion, so that by the
eighteenth century winged windsocks ceased to be thought of as practical possibilities. The final disappearance of the *draco* may be said to date from the time of
Guyot, who mentioned the spectacle of the flying dragon of realistic shape, but
believed that this could be achieved only by supporting it with a pear-kite, from
which the impotent and lifeless creature was to be suspended (Fig. 45).

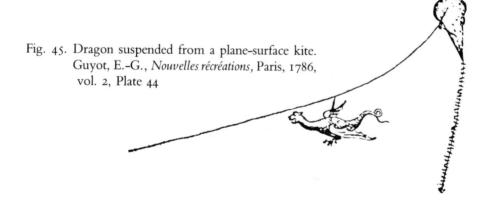

Fig. 45. Dragon suspended from a plane-surface kite.
Guyot, E.-G., *Nouvelles récréations,* Paris, 1786,
vol. 2, Plate 44

While it is quite possible that European kites prior to the sixteenth century arose independently of eastern designs, a diffusionist approach becomes inescapable from at least as early as the mid-sixteenth century. Regular sea-going contacts with southeast Asia, and especially those formed by the Dutch trade routes, were almost certainly responsible for the appearance of a number of kites of various shapes, which rapidly displaced the pennon kites of the previous two centuries. Kites of the lozenge or arch-top kind, still common in Europe today, have for centuries been familiar in south-east Asia, and probably because of their relative ease of construction became more popular in Europe than the old pennon kites had ever been.

The date at which these eastern kites began to be imported is unclear. The first illustration of the new form appears in Jacob Cats' *Alcibiadis,* of 1618 (Plate 25), but a description of a kite of fundamentally similar type is found sixty years earlier in della Porta's *Magia naturalis,*[1] written in 1558, when he was only 22 or 23 years old.

Fig. 46. Seventeenth-century dragon kite. Conrad Meyer, *Sechs und Zwanzig nichtige Kinderspiel,* Zürich, [ca. 1650], plate 12.

[1] della Porta, G. B., *Magiae na. tralis . . . libri iiii,* Neapoli, 1558, pp. 69-70.

Della Porta (1535-1615) was a man of remarkably inquisitive, if also rather gullible, mind. The *Magia naturalis,* reissued in 1589 in greatly expanded form, became one of the best known of the many collections of 'natural wonders' which were so popular in Renaissance times. The description of the kite is somewhat ambiguous, but it is clear that a design in the eastern style, rather than a pennon, is intended. The passage served as the basis for most of what was written about kites for the next hundred years or more:

The Flying Dragon

Also called a comet. Whose construction is as follows: A rectangle should be constructed from very thin rods such that the proportion of length to width is one and a half to one. Two cross pieces are placed within it, either from side to side or from the corners. At their point of intersection a string is attached, and is joined to two others of the same length coming from the ends of the machine. This should be covered with paper or fine linen; and let there be nothing heavy in it. Then from towers, hills, or a high slope, entrust it to the wind when it is blowing evenly and uniformly, not too strongly, which might break the machine, nor too lightly, for if the air is quite calm it will not raise the machine and the stillness of the air renders the labour vain. It should not fly straight, but at an angle, which is effected by pulling on [? *i.e.,* shortening] the string from one end [*i.e.,* the top] and from the other there should be a long tail made of parallel cords with papers tied at regular intervals. When it is sent up with a gentle tug, the artificer to whose hands it is entrusted should not pull it sluggishly or lazily, but powerfully, and thus the flying sail will move up into the air. When it is a little way up (out of the turbulence in the wind caused by the houses) it may be controlled and governed by the hands. Some attach a lantern to it, so that it may look like a comet, while others attach squibs filled with gunpowder, and when it is stationary in the air, a match is sent up the line by means of a ring or some other slippery thing. And this, moving straight up to the sail, sets fire to its mouth, and the machine breaks into many pieces with a great roar, and falls to the ground. Some tie on a kitten or pup and listen to its cries when it has been sent into the air. From this an ingenious man may discover by what means a man might fly with large wings attached to his arms and chest, and little by little from childhood might accustom himself to beating them, from ever higher places. And if anyone should think this extraordinary, let him consider what Archytas the Pythagorean is said to have devised and performed . . .

The description is rather vague, and there is some ambiguity in the wording of the passage about the bridle. The general form of the construction was probably as shown in Figs. 47 and 48, while the bridle was presumably to be attached as in Fig. 49. An inaccurate English translation, published in 1658,[1] does not use the word kite, but gives the literal equivalents of della Porta's terms: 'flying dragon',

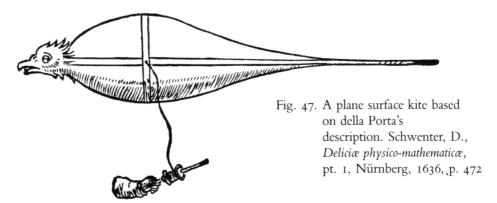

Fig. 47. A plane surface kite based on della Porta's description. Schwenter, D., *Deliciæ physico-mathematicæ*, pt. 1, Nürnberg, 1636, p. 472

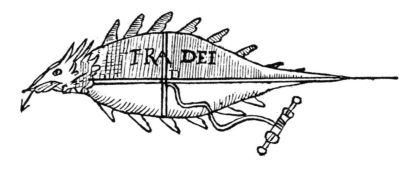

Fig. 48. Another version of della Porta's design. Athanasius Kircher, *Ars magna*, Romae, 1646, pt. 2, p. 826

[1] *Natural Magick . . . in twenty books,* trans. T. Young and S. Speed, London, 1658, p. 409.

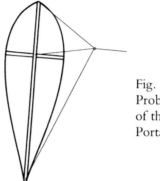

Fig. 49.
Probable attachment
of the bridle on della
Porta's kite

'Comet' and 'flying Sayle'. The inaccuracies are mainly attributable to the transla-
tors' obvious bafflement as to the nature of the object intended. It is unfortunate
that della Porta says nothing about the origin of his *draco volans*, which appears still
to have been a somewhat unusual sight in the mid-sixteenth century. Johannes
Schmidlap, in his manual on the manufacture and use of fireworks,[1] dated in the
Foreword 'New Year's Day, 1560', alludes to the unfamiliarity of kites when he
promises to expand his book for a future edition and to include in it a description of
a *fliegender Trachen,* which, he says, 'the inexperienced think to be an impossibility'.
The association of the kite with fireworks displays, which continues well into the
seventeenth century, suggests, of course, some direct link with the old idea of
putting fire into the windsock standards. In the sixteenth century most kites seem
to have been flown by adults for such purposes, and it was not until somewhat
later that they became the common plaything of children. Brueghel's famous
picture of children at play (1569) contains no kite. The 219th game in the list of 223 in
Chapter 22 of *Gargantua,* 'à la grue', may perhaps refer to kite-flying, a possibility
which is supported by the similarity of the Languedoc word *gruo,* 'kite', but no kite
appears in the 311 games of Fischart's *Gargantua,* of 1575,[2] and the earliest certain
evidence of its use as a plaything in Europe is, once again, the 1618 woodcut in Cats.

Most of the sixteenth and seventeenth century kites in Europe were limited to
the lozenge or pear shapes. The first illustration in an English book, John Bate's

[1] Schmidlap, J., *Künstliche vnd rechtschaffene Fewerwerck zum Schimpff,* Nürnberg, 1564,
A5ᵛ-A6ʳ. (Written about 1560.)

[2] Rausch, H. A., 'Die Spiele der Jugend aus Fischarts Gargantua,' *Jahrbuch für Geschichte,
Sprache, und Literatur Elsass-Lothringens,* vol. 24, 1908, pp. 53ff.

of Fire-workes. 119

Sauciſſons ; betwixt every of which, binde a knot of paper ſhavings, which will make it flye the better ; within a
quarter of a yard of the cloth, let there bee bound a peece
of prepared ſtoupell, the one end whereof, let touch the
cloth , and the other, enter into the end of a Sauciſſon :

Fig. 50. Illustration from John Bate's *The Mysteryes of Nature and Art,* 1634

The Mysteryes of Nature and Art, 1634, depicts a kite of the lozenge type (Fig. 50). This, like so many others at the time, was thought of as an aid to fireworks displays. Bate does not use the word 'kite', but he describes in detail how to make and use one:

How to make fire Drakes

You must take a peece of linnen cloth of a yard or more in length; it must bee cut after the forme of a pane of glasse; fasten two light stickes crosse the same, to make it stand at breadth; then smeare it over with linseed oyle, and liquid varnish tempered together, or else wet it with oyle of peter, and unto the longest corner fasten a match prepared with saltpeter water (as I have taught before) upon which you may fasten divers crackers, or Saucissons; betwixt every of which, binde a knot of paper shavings, which will make it flye the better; within a quarter of a yard of the cloth, let there bee bound a peece of prepared stoupell, the one end whereof, let touch the cloth, and the other enter into the end of a Saucisson: then tie a small rope of length sufficient to rayse it unto what height you shall desire, and to guide it withall: then fire the match, and rayse it against the winde in an open field; and as the match burneth, it will fire the crackers, and saucissons, which will give divers blowes in the ayre; and when the fire is once come unto the stoupell, that will fire the cloth, which will shew very strangely and fearefully.

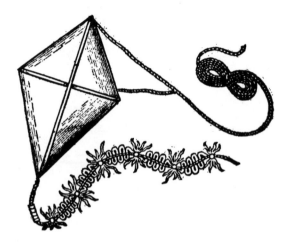

Fig. 51. Another illustration of Bate's kite, showing the 'Saucissons' more clearly.
(In Bate it is printed upside-down)

The slightly more complex pear-kite is illustrated in Babington's *Pyrotechnia*,[1] where it is used to 'represent the Sphere, moving in the ayre, without any other supportation':

Cause a Sphere to bee made somewhat light, and on the horizon place your rockets, and in the zenith or upper part, let there bee a pinne passe thorow the meridian, with a ring fastned to it, to hang it by; this must bee fastned to a large Kite, so as the Sphere may hang six foot under it, then fasten a match of cotton to the nose of the first rocket, and light it, which having done, raise your Kite, and by such time as it is at the highest, the rockets shall take fire, and shall cause it to make divers revolutions in the ayre; you may place the midst of this sphere full of lights, which will seeme very strange.

[1] Babington, J., *Pyrotechnia*, London, 1635, pp. 44-6.

This passage contains what appears to be the first printed use of the word 'kite'. Babington uses it, however, without explanation or comment, from which we may assume that both the object and its name had been familiar in England for some time before 1635. The design is the standard pear, but no bridle is used (Plate 27).

Although the lozenge and pear shapes were the basic structures, they were often varied by shaping of the edges of the paper, which was sometimes done very elegantly. Fig. 47 is from Schwenter (1636), while Fig. 48, based on Schwenter, is from Athanasius Kircher's *Ars magna*.[1] Kircher was, of course, deeply interested in the east, but his knowledge of it had no obvious effects on his discussion of the kite. The design, and the uses to which he suggested it be put, are standard for seventeenth-century Europe, and are in any case largely dependent on material from Schwenter. As in the case of della Porta's design, the outer edges of these kites are made of light reeds, while the crossed sticks give rigidity to the structure. Whether this form of kite is a European modification, or reflects eastern practice, is uncertain, but it is possible that it was influenced by the earlier generation of European kites exemplified in Vienna codex 3064.

Kircher's comments on the uses to which kites may be put are rather more extensive than those to be found in most other books of the period:

> Due to the invention of this device certain of our Fathers in India were rescued from great peril at the hands of the barbarians. They were being held in prison and at a loss to know how to free themselves from captivity. One of them, cleverer than the rest, invented a machine of this sort, first threatening the barbarians that, unless they delivered his friends, portentous things would soon be seen and they would feel the manifest wrath of the gods. The barbarians laughed at this; but he made a kite out of very fine paper, in the middle of which he attached a mixture of sulphur, pitch, and wax, so that on being ignited the device would be illuminated and display the words IRA DEI in their own language for them to read. Next he attached a tail to the device and launched it into the air. Soon a wind caught it, and it flew off with the terrifying appearance of a fiery dragon.
>
> The barbarians, seeing the extraordinary movement of the apparition, were thunderstruck and, remembering the words of the Fathers, were afraid that they were about to suffer the predicted punishment. They therefore quickly opened the

---

[1] Kircher, A., *Ars magna lucis et umbrae*, Rome, 1646, Part 2, p. 826.

prison and allowed their captives to go free. Meanwhile the device caught fire with a report, as if to show its approval, and fell motionless of its own accord. Hence the Fathers, by means of spectacles of nature, achieved what gold had failed to do, merely through the inspiration of fear. . . .

Anyone who has a falcon trained to obey its master's voice can work the most amazing tricks: if he tie the string to the falcon's foot, he can direct the aforesaid machine in any direction at command, and so by this means achieve quite prodigious effects.

The last comment is one of the earliest and certainly the most unusual suggestion for controlling the movement of a kite. Allowing a bird to fly from the end of a string was of course a common practice—see the Middelburg picture. The idea of tying the bird to the kite itself and flying both in tandem is most ingenious. Later Kircher makes a further suggestion:

On the Ascension Day of Christ our Lord angels may with little effort be shown flying through the air. An arrangement of whistles around the edges of the machine will greatly increase the wonder of these spectacles; set going by the movement of the air they will produce a sweet harmonious sound, especially if little bells are also attached. . . .

In a concluding passage he moves away from his simple plane-surface kite to discuss the old idea of a hollow dragon-kite:

If you wish to display various nocturnal spectacles, you may make a hollow kite from dense and opaque but very light material. In the bottom and sides should be cut the shapes of the things that you wish to represent, and these re-covered with very fine paper steeped in oil. When candles are set inside, the shape of the animal will thus shine through. If you want to present a truly portentous spectacle, cut out letters which, when the candles inside are lit, will be legible in the darkness. It is barely possible to indicate how much terror and wonder a spectacle of this kind produces. . . .

In the sixteenth century the kite had still been something of a prodigy; by the seventeenth it was altogether commonplace. Butler mentions kites in *Hudibras,* and seems to take them for granted:

It happen'd as a boy, one night,
Did fly his tarcel of a kite;

·   ·   ·

His train was six yards long, milk-white,
At th' end of which, there hung a light,
Inclos'd in lanthorn made of paper . . .

Francesco Lana, in his *Prodromo* (Brescia, 1670, p. 50), mentions that kites were commonly flown by the children of Italy in his day. In England, once again, Isaac Newton is said to have played with kites when he was a boy, and is even credited with having made some improvements in their design:

> . . . he introduced the flying of paper kites, and he is said to have investigated their best forms and proportions as well as the number and position of the points to which the string should be attached. He constructed also lanterns of crimpled paper, in which he placed a candle, to light him to school in the dark winter mornings; and in dark nights he tied them to the tails of his kites in order to terrify the country people, who took them for comets . . . even when he was occupied

LA MERELLE, & LE CERF VOLANT

La Merelle et Franc du quareau   *& l'autre avec son Cerf Volant*
Sont icy mis sur le bureau,   *va courant a perte d'haleine*
chacun a bien joüer prend peine ;   *pour fournir d'vn joüet au Vent* 17

Fig. 52. Rectangular kite from J. Stella, *Les Ieux et plaisirs de l'enfance*, Paris, 1657, plate 17.

with his paper kites he was endeavouring to find out the proper form of a body which would experience the least resistance when moving in a fluid.[1]

As far as I can discover, however, the only mention of a kite in a strictly scientific context during the seventeenth century occurs in a pair of tantalizing entries in an undated note-sheet of Robert Hooke's:

> To Discover Land at a Destance by a glasse Raisd by a kite to a great height.
> Things worthy tryall at a great height in ye air as kite.

There is, unfortunately, no record of any actual kite experiments by that very inquisitive empiricist.[2] It was not until the following century that European scientists discovered something of the kite's potentiality as an instrument of investigation.

As it is now clear that kites have been known in Europe for rather longer than was once thought to have been the case, one may well ask whether at any time they were considered as a potential means of human flight. Man-lifting kites, which were developed by nineteenth-century inventors for a variety of applications, had long been known in the east. Were they used in medieval or Renaissance Europe? In 1646, Kircher suggested that kites could lift a man; in 1558 they had made della Porta think of winged flight; and in the fifteenth century both the kites flown by the writer of Vienna codex 3064 and the *dracones* brandished by Kyeser's knights must have exerted a pull sufficient to suggest man-lifting possibilities. Despite these hints, there appear to be no western reports of man-lifters, either real or imaginary, before modern times.

During the late sixteenth and seventeenth centuries the passage from della Porta was frequently quoted and paraphrased, but the idea that the kite might be used as the basis of a flying machine never seems to have caught the imagination of experimenters or theoreticians. Not only are there no reports of man-lifters, but

---

[1] Brewster, Sir David, *Life of Sir Isaac Newton,* 2 vols., Edinburgh, 1855, Vol. 1, pp. 11, 16.
[2] Royal Society Library, classified papers, Vol. 20, item 54, recto. See also Hubbard, T. O'B., 'British Aeronautics in the 17th Century', *Aeronautics* (London), Vol. 4, October 1911, p.186, and *The Diary of Robert Hooke,* ed. H. W. Robinson and W. Adams, London, 1935, p.146, in which Hooke mentions Wren's idea that human flight might be achieved by the use of kites.

important books like Flayder's *De arte volandi*[1] and Wilkins' *Mathematicall Magick*[2] ignore the kite entirely. In view of its many potentialities, the neglect of the kite in the seventeenth century is especially unfortunate, but as the increase in its familiarity coincided with its relegation to the status of a toy, such a failure of response among the scientists and technicians was probably inevitable. Not until Cayley made his little glider in 1804 did the kite re-assume its important role in aeronautics.

[1] Flayder, F. H., *De arte volandi* . . ., [Tübingen,] 1627.
[2] Wilkins, J., *Mathematicall Magick; or, the wonders that may be performed by mechanicall geometry,* London, 1648, pp. 191-223.

5 | The Eighteenth Century and Electric Kites

Among children, kites continued to increase in popularity during the eighteenth century. Miss Bayne-Powell writes: 'Kite-flying, though it never became the sport that it is in China and Japan, was very popular in the eighteenth century, indeed we find in many pictures of fields and open spaces, the figure of a boy flying a kite.'[1] In France the sport aroused such interest that the authorities were forced, on October 16, 1736, to forbid for a time the flying of kites in public places, due to riots which had broken out between contending fliers.

It was, however, the use of the kite by physicists and meteorologists that really began the long process of development which continued until the early twentieth century. The earliest application of the European kite for scientific purposes seems to have been the work of Alexander Wilson, in 1749. The claim establishing Wilson's priority was not published until many years later, but there seems to be no reason to doubt the truth of the account. The following description contains the first known mention of 'flying in train', or attaching more than one kite to the same line. Unfortunately, however, it contains no indication of the shape of the kites used, though we may probably assume that they were of the diamond or pear variety, both of which remained popular during the eighteenth century:

> Among the more advanced students, who, in the years 1748 and 1749, attended the lectures on Divinity in the University, was Mr Thomas Melvill. . . . With this young person Mr Wilson then lived in the closest intimacy. Of several philo-sophical schemes which occurred to them in their social hours, Mr Wilson proposed one, which was to explore the temperature of the atmosphere in the higher regions, by raising a number of paper kites, one above another, upon the

[1] Bayne-Powell, R., *The English Child in the Eighteenth Century*, London, 1939, p. 218.

same line, with thermometers appended to those that were to be most elevated. Though they expected, in general, that kites thus connected might be raised to an unusual height, still they were somewhat uncertain how far the thing might succeed upon trial. But the thought being quite new to them, and the purpose to be gained of some importance, they began to prepare for the experiment in the spring of 1749.

Mr Wilson's home at Camlachie was the scene of all the little bustle which now became necessary; and both Mr Melvill and he, alike dexterous in the use of their hands, found much amusement in going through the preliminary work, till,

Fig. 53. Child's kite in eighteenth-century Germany. Chodowiecki (1726–1801).
A four-leg bridle appears to be used

at last, they finished half-a-dozen large paper-kites, from four to seven feet in height, upon the strongest, and, at the same time, upon the slightest construction the materials would admit of. They had also been careful, in giving orders, early, for a very considerable quantity of line, to be spun of such different sizes and strength, as they judged would best answer their purpose; so that one fine day, about the middle of July, when favoured by a gentle steady breeze, they brought out their whole apparatus into an adjoining field, amidst a numerous company, consisting of their friends and others, whom the rumour of this new and ingenious project had drawn from the town.

They began with raising the smallest kite, which, being exactly balanced, soon mounted steadily to its utmost limit, carrying up a line very slender, but of a strength sufficient to command it. In the mean time, the second kite was made ready. Two assistants supported it between them in a sloping direction, with its breast to the wind, and with its tail laid out evenly upon the ground behind, whilst a third person, holding part of its line tight in his hand, stood at a good distance directly in front. Things being ordered, the extremity of the line belonging to the kite already in the air, was hooked to a loop at the back of the second, which being now let go, mounted very superbly, and in a little time also took up as much line as could be supported with advantage; thereby allowing its companion to soar to an elevation proportionally higher.

Upon launching these kites according to the method which had been projected, and affording them abundance of proper line, the uppermost one ascended to an amazing height, disappearing at times among the white summer clouds, whilst all the rest, in a series, formed with it, in the air below, such a lofty scale, and that, too, affected by such regular and conspiring motion, as at once changed a boyish pastime into a spectacle which greatly interested every beholder. The pressure of the breeze upon so many surfaces communicating with one another, was found too powerful for a single person to withstand, when contending with the undermost strong line, and it became therefore necessary to keep the mastery over the kites by other means.

This species of aërial machinery answering so well, Mr Wilson and Mr Melvill employed it several times during that and the following summer, in pursuing those atmospherical experiments for which the kites had been originally intended. To obtain the information they wanted, they contrived that thermometers, properly secured, and having bushy tassels of paper tied to them, should be let fall at stated periods from some of the higher kites; which was accomplished by the gradual singeing of a match-line.

When engaged in these experiments, though now and then they communicated immediately with the clouds, yet, as this happened always in fine weather, no symptoms whatever of an electrical nature came under their observation. The sublime analysis of the thunder-bolt, and of the electricity of the atmosphere, lay yet entirely undiscovered, and was reserved two years longer for the sagacity of the celebrated Dr Franklin. In a letter from Mr Melvill to Mr Wilson, dated at Geneva, 1st April 1753, we find, among several other particulars, his curiosity highly excited by the fame of the Philadelphian experiment; and a great ardour expressed for prosecuting such researches by the advantage of their combined kites. But, in the December following, this beloved companion of Mr Wilson was removed by death. . . .[1]

[1] Wilson, P., 'Biographical Account of Alexander Wilson', *Transactions of the Royal Society of Edinburgh*, Vol. 10, 1826, pp. 284–7.

17. Standard, probably a windsock. Porcelain dish, Chinese, mark of Ch'eng-hua
(1465-87), period of K'ang-
hsi (1662-1722). *Fitzwilliam
Museum*, C.33-1931

18. Fire-breathing windsock
standard. St Gallen, Stifts-
bibliothek, codex 22, *Psalterium aureum*, p. 140, ninth
century AD

19. The *draco volans*, plane-
surface kite. Conrad
Kyeser, *Bellifortis*. Göttingen, Niedersächsische
Staats- und Universitätsbibliothek, codex philos. 63, f.
105ʳ, 1405.

20a–f. Versions of the *draco*, with and without wings, shown as both plane-surface
and three-dimensional. In 20c an attempt has been made to show the bridle.
All from the fifteenth century.

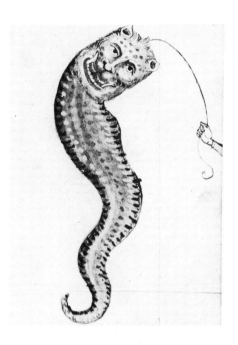

21. Pennon kite in Vienna,
    Österreichische Nationalbib-
    liothek, codex 3064, f. 6^r, *ca.*
    1430.

22. Modern reconstruction of
    the pennon kite.

23. Snake kite from Cam-
    bodia. Its structure is very
    similar to that of mediaeval
    European pennon kites.

24. Icon, St Nicholas' Church,
    Nizhni-Novgorod, show-
    ing what is probably a
    pennon-kite, top right.

25. First European illustration of a kite of lozenge shape. J. Cats, *Silenus Alcibiades*, Middelburg, 1618, opposite p. 106.

27. Pear kite in Babington's *Pyrotechnia*, 1635.

26. Another version of the kite in Plate 25. J. Cats, *Houwelyck*, 1628, A3.

28, 29. Arch-top kite from *Stories of Instruction and Delight*, 1802.

30. De Romas' experiments with a pigeon and a dog.

31, 32. Baden-Powell's 36 ft. man-lifter, 1894.

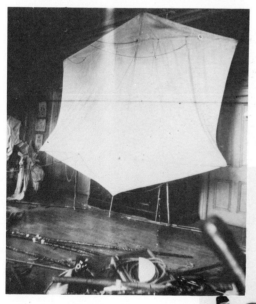

33. Baden-Powell's 12 ft.
'levitor' kite, 1895.

34. Early ascent in Baden-
Powell's apparatus.

35. Baden-Powell, centre, with one of his 'levitor' kites.

36. Walter Russell Magoun in a man-lifting kite, USA, 1910.

37. Gyro-kite by Charles Chubb. *Smithsonian Institution*

38. Eddy's daughter, Margaret, with some of her father's kites.

39. Another photograph of Eddy's kites, showing one of the frames.

40. A modern Eddy kite, 9 ft. X 9 ft., held by Philip David Hart.

The Franklin experiment, mentioned above, is no doubt the most famous of all scientific applications of the kite. It took place at some time during June 1752. For this purpose Franklin used a 'common kite' which was apparently very similar to the one depicted in Bate's book (see Fig. 50).

The only contemporary description of the experiment itself is by Priestley, who apparently had the details direct from Franklin. He says, in part:

> . . . he took the opportunity of the first approaching thunder storm to take a walk into a field, in which there was a shed convenient for his purpose. But dreading the ridicule which too commonly attends unsuccessful attempts in science, he communicated his intended experiment to no body but his son, who assisted him in raising the kite.
>
> The kite being raised, a considerable time elapsed before there was any appearance of its being electrified. One very promising cloud had passed over it without any effect; when, at length, just as he was beginning to despair of his contrivance, he observed some loose threads of the hempen string to stand erect, and to avoid one another, just as if they had been suspended on a common conductor. Struck with this promising appearance, he immediately presented his knuckle to the key, and (let the reader judge of the exquisite pleasure he must have felt at that moment) the discovery was complete. He perceived a very evident electric spark. Others succeeded, even before the string was wet, so as to put the matter past all dispute, and when the rain had wet the string, he collected electric fire very copiously. This happened in June 1752, a month after the electricians in France had verified the same theory, but before he heard of any thing they had done.[1]

Shortly after the experiment, Franklin gave instructions as to how it might be repeated:

> Make a small Cross of two light Strips of Cedar, the Arms so long as to reach to the four Corners of a large thin Silk Handkerchief when extended; tie the Corners of the Handkerchief to the Extremities of the Cross, so you have the Body of a Kite; which being properly accommodated with a Tail, Loop and String, will rise in the Air, like those made of Paper; but this being of Silk is fitter to bear the Wet and Wind of a Thunder Gust without tearing. To the Top of the upright Stick of the Cross is to be fixed a very sharp pointed Wire, rising a Foot or more above the Wood. To the End of the Twine, next the Hand, is to be tied a silk Ribbon, and where the Twine and the silk join, a Key may be fastened. This Kite is to be raised when a Thunder Gust appears to be coming on, and the Person

[1] Priestley, J., *History and Present State of Electricity*, London, 1767, pp. 171–2.

who holds the String must stand within a Door, or Window, or under some Cover, so that the Silk Ribbon may not be wet; and Care must be taken that the Twine does not touch the Frame of the Door or Window. As soon as any of the Thunder Clouds come over the Kite, the pointed Wire will draw the Electric Fire from them, and the Kite, with all the Twine, will be electrified, and the loose Filaments of the Twine will stand out every Way, and be attracted by an approaching Finger. And when the Rain has wet the Kite and Twine, so that it can conduct the Electric Fire freely, you will find it stream out plentifully from the Key on the Approach of your Knuckle. At this Key the Phial may be charg'd; and from Electric Fire thus obtain'd, Spirits may be kindled, and all the other Electric Experiments be perform'd, which are usually done by the Help of a rubbed Glass Globe or Tube; and thereby the *Sameness* of the Electric Matter with that of Lightning compleatly demonstrated.[1]

Franklin's claim to have invented the electric kite did not go undisputed. De Romas, a scientist from Nérac, had apparently thought of the idea before Franklin's experiment took place, but he failed to put it into effect until too late. In great distress at having been forestalled in his invention, de Romas published a book in which he sought to establish that the priority was morally his.

De Romas's kite was of the 'pear' variety which, according to Lecornu,[2] is the oldest shape known in France. He attempted to repeat Franklin's demonstration on May 14, 1753, but was unsuccessful, due to his using a line with too high an electrical resistance. He accordingly wrapped the line with copper wire and tried again, on June 7, 1753, during a storm. This time the experiment was spectacularly successful, producing sparks seven or eight inches long. The line used on that occasion was 780 feet long. Later, using a 1,100 foot line, de Romas claimed to have produced sparks six, ten, and as much as eighteen feet in length.

Some years later de Romas carried out some extraordinary manœuvres with his electric kite, during which he preserved the life of a terrified pigeon, but managed to kill a large dog:

> During a violent storm . . . I raised my kite. Near the lower end of the string, that is, near the place where it was tied to the silk thread, I placed on the ground a tripod made of three brass wires, each eighteen inches long and as thick as a pen,

[1] Franklin, B., *The Papers of Benjamin Franklin*, ed. L. W. Labaree, Vol. 4, New Haven, 1961, pp. 360-9.

[2] Lecornu, J., *Les Cerfs-volants*, Paris, 1902, p. 45.

and meeting in a point at one end. Between the feet of this tripod, and approximately in the middle, I placed a glass vessel eleven inches high and five inches in diameter, and whose mouth was sufficiently wide to allow the introduction of a hand. At the bottom of this vessel I cemented . . . one end of a silk cord. At the other end of this I tied a pigeon by the neck, so that it could not escape from the cell which, in accordance with my plan, must remain open. Finally, at the point of the tripod I attached one end of a metal chain, the other end of which I allowed to pass into the interior of the vessel, being careful, however, that the length of the chain was such that it hung an inch over the head of the bird.

At the sight of these preparations, the people who had gathered to watch my operations, and who were soon frightened by several spontaneous flashes of electricity which they were not expecting, presaged the imminent death of the pigeon.

Fig. 54. Common pear-kites

I directed about twenty flashes of electricity [from the kite] . . . on to the point of the tripod, but the pigeon showed only fear at each flash, and remained safe and sound.

. . . Several feet away from the tripod . . . I drove a stake into the ground . . . To this I tied a dog with a strong silk cord. Having done that . . . I waited until the storm had so abated that the kite line was giving off sparks only three or four inches in length . . . As soon as this happened . . . I directed a single such spark at the head of the dog; and the animal immediately fell dead to the ground.[1]

[1] de Romas, J., *Mémoire, sur les moyens de se garantir de la foudre dans les maisons*, Bordeaux, 1776, pp. 87–9. (My translation.)

Plate 30 illustrates de Romas's pear-kite, showing the balancing tassels at the ends of the wings. The woodcut is from de Romas's book.

Due to the spectacular experiment at Nérac, de Romas gained the reputation of being a kind of sorcerer. This reputation followed him to Bordeaux, where he went in 1759 to demonstrate his lightning-kite to a more august audience, and where he was the victim of a remarkable and unfortunate coincidence. The experiment was to have been carried out in a public garden. While he waited for suitable weather, de Romas left his kite with a café-proprietor, whose premises were situated on a terrace in the gardens. Many of the inhabitants, ignorantly believing the kite itself to be the cause of the atmospheric electricity, became nervous, as they feared a thunderbolt. A storm blew up and lightning did in fact hit the café. The inhabitants, no longer in any doubt, threatened to destroy everything if the kite were not handed over to them. The proprietor was understandably terrified; he complied, and the kite was promptly torn to shreds.

A great many investigators followed Franklin and de Romas in the use of the 'electric kite'. Among these were Fr. Beccaria of Turin, Prince Gallitzin and Dentan at the Hague, and Pilâtre de Rozier, celebrated as the first balloonist. A Dutch physicist, Peter van Musschenbroek, described experiments made during 1756–7, of which the following is one account. (Musschenbroek, like de Romas, used animals as subjects, but they seem to have fared rather better than de Romas's unfortunate dog.)

> On the 20th July, 1757, after a violent storm had broken out about 7 o'clock in the evening, I flew a kite. The steel wire immediately gave off very strong explosions. Sometimes these occurred at the same time as the flashes of lightning, but they ceased when the thunder could be heard. They succeeded one another with the greatest rapidity, producing a noise that could be heard at a great distance. When I brought the wire near the heads of a dog, a buck, and a young bull, these animals were struck so violently that they immediately took flight and were not keen to have the experiment repeated.[1]

Musschenbroek also included in his book a brief mathematical description of the system of forces which cause a kite to fly.[2] He and his celebrated contemporary, Leonhard Euler, were among the first scientists to attempt such mathematical

----

[1] Musschenbroek, P. van, *Introductio ad philosophiam naturalem*, Leyden, 1762, Vol. I, pp. 295–6. (My translation.)

[2] *Ibid.*, p. 177.

expositions. It was not, however, until the well-known meteorologist C. F. Marvin published a series of articles in the *Monthly Weather Review*[1] at the end of the nineteenth century that a complete treatment of the subject appeared.

One other experimenter with electric kites deserves special mention. This is Tiberius Cavallo, who has left us one of the most comprehensive and detailed accounts. The following passage gives a very clear idea of the techniques involved and the results to be expected:

> The first instrument that I made use of, to observe the Electricity of the atmosphere, was an electrical kite, which I had constructed, not with a view to observe the Electricity of the air, for this, I thought, was very weak and seldom to be observed; but as an instrument, which could be occasionally used in time of a thunder-storm, in order to observe the Electricity of the clouds. The kite however being just finished, together with its string, which contained a brass wire through its whole length, I raised it the 31st of August 1775, at seven of the clock in the afternoon, the weather being a little cloudy, and the wind just sufficient for the purpose. The extremity of the string being insulated, I applied my fingers to it, which, contrary to my expectation, drew very vivid, and pungent sparks: I charged a coated phial at the string several times; but I did not then observe the quality of the Electricity. This successful experiment induced me to raise the kite very often, and to keep it up, for several hours together, thinking that if any periodical Electricity, or any change of its quality took place in the atmosphere, it might very probably be discovered by this instrument . . .
>
> The first electrical kite, that I constructed, was seven feet high, and it was made of paper with a stick or straiter, and a cane bow, like the kites commonly used by school-boys. On the upper part of the straiter I fixed an iron spike, projecting about a foot above the kite, which, I then thought, was absolutely necessary to collect the Electricity, and I covered the paper of the kite with turpentine, in order to defend it from the rain. This kite, perfect as I thought it to be, in its construction, and fit for the experiments, for which it was intended, soon manifested its imperfections, and after being raised a few times, it became quite unfit for farther use; it being so large, and consequently heavy, that it could not be used, except when the wind was strong, and then after much trouble in raising and drawing it in, it often received some damage, which soon obliged me to construct other kites upon a different plan, in order to ascertain which method would answer the best for my purpose. I gradually lessened their size, and varied their form, till I observed upon trial, that a common school-boy's kite, was as good an electrical kite as mine. In

[1] Republished as Marvin, C. F., *The Mechanics and Equilibrium of Kites*, Washington, 1897. This exhaustive monograph is a model of scientific method.

consequence of which I constructed my kites in the most simple manner, and in nothing different from the children's kites, except that I covered them with varnish, or with well boiled linseed oil, in order to defend them from the rain, and I covered the back part of the straiter with tin-foil, which however has not the least power to increase its Electricity. I also furnish the upper extremity of the straiter with a slender wire pointed, which, in time of a thunder-storm, may perhaps draw the Electricity from the clouds, somewhat more effectually; but, in general, I find, . . . that it does not in the least affect the Electricity at the string. The kites, that I generally have used, are about four feet high, and little above two feet wide. This size, I find, is the most convenient, because it renders them easy to be managed, and at the same time they can draw a sufficient quantity of string. As for silk or linen kites, they require a good deal of wind to be raised, and then they are not so cheap nor so easy to be made, as paper kites are. The string sometimes breaks, and the kite is lost, or broken, for which reason, these kites should be made as cheap and as simple as possible.

The string is the most material part of this apparatus; for the Electricity produced is more or less, according as the string is a better, or a worse Conductor. The string, which I made for my large kite, consisted of two threads of common twine twisted together with a brass wire between the strands. This string served very well for two, or three trials, but on examination, I soon found that the wire in it was broken in many places, and it was continually snapping; the metallic continuation therefore being so soon interrupted, the string became soon so bad, that it acted nothing better than common twine without a wire. I attempted to mend it, by joining the broken pieces of wire, and working into the twine, another wire, which proved a very laborious work; but the remedy had very little effect, the wire breaking again after the first trial, which determined me to adopt other methods; and after several experiments, I found that the best string was one, which I made by twisting a copper thread with two very thin threads of twine. . . .

In raising the kite when the weather is very cloudy and rainy, in which time there is fear of meeting with great quantity of Electricity, I generally use to hang upon the string . . . the hook of a chain . . ., the other extremity of which falls upon the ground. Sometimes I use another caution besides, which is to stand upon an insulating stool; in which situation, I think, that if any great quantity of Electricity, suddenly discharged by the clouds, strikes the kite, it cannot much affect my person. As to insulated reels, and such like instruments, that some gentlemen have used for to raise the kite, without danger of receiving any shock; fit for the purpose as they may appear to be in theory, they are yet very inconvenient to be managed. Except the kite be raised in time of a thunder-storm, there is no great danger for the Operator to receive any shock. Although I have raised my electrical kite hundreds of times without any caution whatever, I have very seldom received a few exceedingly slight shocks in my arms. In time of a thunder-storm, if the kite has not been raised before, I would not advise a person to raise it while the stormy clouds are just overhead; the danger in such time being very great, even with the precautions above mentioned. . . .[1]

(Later Cavallo also demonstrated that it is the string rather than the kite itself that collects the electricity.)

The kites used by the eighteenth-century investigators were usually cumbersome and inefficient. Tailless kites were still unknown in Europe (except perhaps on the Dutch coast) and the lines, especially those used for conducting electricity, were thick and heavy. It is not surprising that the kites did not fly to very great heights. An elevation of 500 feet was the usual maximum for a single kite, a poor performance which was not substantially bettered until the great period of development of the meteorological kite at the end of the next century.

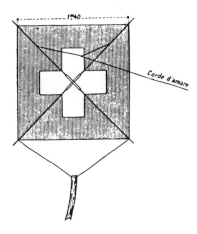

Fig. 55. Swiss signal kite, 1883.

[1] Cavallo, T., *A Complete Treatise on Electricity*, London, 1777, pp. 330–8.

6 | Meteorological Kites

It was not until quite late in the nineteenth century that kites were used regularly for meteorological observations. Soon after the establishment of full-time weather bureaus, kites began to be employed for obtaining detailed records of the upper atmosphere, but for a century after the attempts of Wilson, Franklin, and de Romas, very little interest was taken in their potentialities. This was almost certainly due to the crudity of western kites before the work of Eddy, Hargrave, and their successors. Kites were inefficient, fragile, and awkward, and were encumbered by long tails. Nevertheless, on a number of occasions before the end of the century, investigators tolerated these disadvantages in order to discover what further information kites might be able to provide.

Perhaps the first serious application of the kite in the nineteenth century was in the work of Captain Parry and the Reverend George Fisher at Igloolik, during Parry's second voyage, 1822–23. They wanted to make observations which would determine the law of variation of the temperature of the atmosphere according to height above sea-level in very cold regions. For this purpose they used a paper kite to which was attached a Six's thermometer. In what must have been one of the coldest kite-flyings in history, Fisher and the Captain raised their kite to a measured height of 379 feet. (They believed that the unrecorded height exceeded 400 feet.) The temperature at ground level was −24°, but they stood patiently for fifteen minutes, waiting for the thermometer to readjust. The experiment, although valuable in itself, cannot have exhilarated the men with its results, since no variation of temperature whatever was recorded.[1]

[1] Abbe, C., 'The Kite Used in 1822 by Fisher', *Monthly Weather Review*, Vol. 25, No. 4, April 1897, pp. 163–4.

In the autumn of 1827, Colladon, then a very young man, flew a train of three common French pear-kites near Geneva, using about four hundred yards of line, in an attempt to repeat Franklin's experiment. He was remarkably successful, producing sparks a yard long which flashed around a room in the parental home, causing his aged father some dismay. In later years Colladon wrote an amusing account of his experiment but no scientific information of any value seems to have been drawn from it.[1]

Until this time no one had thought of putting kite-flying on an organized basis. In the 1830s, however, some Americans gathered together for this purpose. They were the members of what was known as the Franklin Kite Club. The following description of the club and its activities is by William J. Rhees, once Chief Clerk of the Smithsonian Institution:

> In 1835–36 several gentlemen formed a society with the name of 'The Franklin Kite Club' for the purpose of making electrical experiments. For a considerable time they met once a week at the City Hospital grounds [in Philadelphia] and flew their kites. These were generally square in shape, made of muslin or silk, stretched over a framework of cane reeds, varying in size from 6 feet upward, some being 20 feet square. For flying the kites, annealed copper wire was used, wound upon a heavy reel 2 or 3 feet in diameter, insulated by being placed on glass supports. When one kite was up sometimes a number of others would be sent up on the same string. The reel being inside the fence the wire from the kite crossed over the road. Upon one occasion as a cartman passed, gazing at the kites he stopped directly under the wire and was told to catch hold of it and see how hard it pulled. In order to reach it he stood up on his cart, putting one foot on the horse's back. When he touched the wire the shock went through him, as also the horse, causing the latter to jump and the man to turn a somersault, much to the amusement of the lookers on. . . .[2]

The Club also practised kite-flying for recreational purposes, using decorative kites imported from China.[3] In good skating weather sleds were drawn, and on one

[1] Colladon, D., 'Expériences sur les cerfs-volants', *La Nature*, Vol. 15, No. 757, July 16, 1887, pp. 97–9.

[2] Abbe, C., 'The Franklin Kite Club', *Monthly Weather Review*, Vol. 24, No. 11, November 1896, p. 416. See also Swaim, J., 'Electro-Meteorological Observations', *The American Journal of Science and Arts*, 1st s., Vol. 32, No. 2, July 1837, pp. 304–7.

[3] Abbe, C., 'Espy and the Franklin Kite Club', *Monthly Weather Review*, Vol. 24, No. 9, September 1896, p. 334.

occasion they revived an old custom by launching a kitten in a basket. (It was subsequently landed safely by parachute.)

Espy, the well-known American meteorologist and author of *The Philosophy of Storms*, was a member of the Club and used kites to investigate the properties of columnar clouds. In one of his comments on this matter he quotes from J. N. Nicollet, who mentions that kites flown by Club-members were made to rise nearly perpendicularly when columnar clouds passed over them, while elsewhere Espy relates some of his own experiences with kites:

> I would recommend that gentlemen residing in mountainous districts, where the clouds sometimes form on the sides of the mountains, should ascertain the perpendicular heights of these clouds at their bases and see whether they are 100 yards high for every degree of Fahrenheit by which the temperature of the air is above the dew-point at the moment of formation . . . Since writing the above a kite was sent up into the base of a cloud and its height ascertained by the sextant and compared with the height calculated from the dew-point, allowing 100 yards for every degree by which the dew-point was below the temperature of the air, and the agreement of the two methods was within the limits of the errors of observation. In this case the base of the cloud was over 1,200 yards high. Moreover, the motions of the kite whenever a forming cloud came nearly over it proved that there was an upmoving column of air under it. I speak of cumulus clouds in the form of sugar loaves with flat bases.
>
> When the kite experiments mentioned before were performed and the kite was allowed to stay up in the air many hundred yards high in the night, by touching with the hand the reel on which the wire was wound which was attached to the kite, the *fingers became luminous*, quite brilliant, though no sensation of shock was produced; but by touching the wire itself a very pungent shock was experienced; and one day in particular when the kite entered the base of a forming cloud the discharge of electricity down the wire, snapping to an iron conductor stuck in the ground, terminating at its upper end within an inch or two of the wire, became fearful . . . indeed the shock on touching the wire became quite sharp when the kite was elevated a few hundred feet, even in a clear sky.[1]

At about the period of Espy's experiments, W. R. Birt was working at Kew Observatory, in England. Assisted by Sir Francis Reynolds, he tried ordinary children's kites to ascertain whether they might be of use in making meteorological observations. As the uncertainty of movement of such kites proved them, however, to be unsatisfactory, he and Reynolds experimented instead with 'an excellent

[1] Espy, J. P., *The Philosophy of Storms*, Boston, 1841, pp. 167, 175.

hexagonal kite of Mr Birt's construction'. This was held fast by means of three cords, one attached 'in the usual manner' (presumably to a three-leg bridle joining the centre and top two corners), and by two others, one fixed to each 'wing'. The three cords were then pegged to the apices of an equilateral triangle laid out on the ground. Tension on the side-cords regulated the kite's attitude and gave it great lifting power (Fig. 56). These experiments took place on August 14, 1847.[1] Birt suggested that kites be used extensively in meteorology, and pointed out the ease with which measuring instruments might be raised and lowered by means of a block and tackle. Nothing, however, seems to have come of the idea,[2] though Birt's

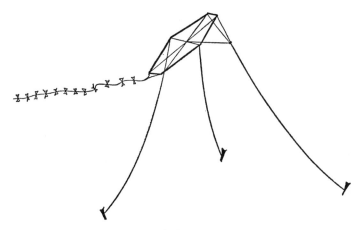

Fig. 56. Birt's kite at Kew, 1847

method of controlling his kite may have come to the notice of Maillot, whose man-lifter (Fig. 63) is remarkably similar.

Birt also suggested that large hexagonal kites, if made of silk and coated with an elastic varnish, could be of use in military as well as civil applications. More than half a century later kites did, in fact, acquire military significance (see Chapter 10).

Other occasional experimenters with meteorological kites during the nineteenth

[1] 'Experiments made at the Kew Observatory on a new Kite-Apparatus for Meteorological Observations, or other purposes', *The London, Edinburgh, and Dublin Philosophical Magazine and Journal of Science*, Vol. 31, No. 207, September 1847, pp. 191–2.

[2] A suggestion for the meteorological use of kites was made in Russia in 1846 by Professor A. Popov, of Moscow and Kazan. The idea created some interest, but appears never to have been put into effect.

century included Cleveland Abbe in America (1867 and 1876),[1] Fr. van Rysselbergh in Belgium (1880), and a Frenchman, Hervé-Mangon. The last experimented with instrument-carrying kites towards the end of the 1870s and was directly responsible for encouraging an important investigator, Charles du Hauvel, to begin theoretical work on the requirements of a meteorological kite. A British meteorologist, E. D. Archibald, must, however, be credited with initiating the use of the kite as a serious meteorological tool–a use which continued into the 1930s. He began work in November 1883, his principal object being to measure the increase in wind velocity with increasing elevation.[2] Previously the perfecting of the balloon had absorbed most of the attention of scientists working on this subject. Balloons were often unsatisfactory, however, in that, if they were free, the recovery of the instruments was difficult, while if they were captive (that is, retained to the ground by means of a line), lateral winds tended to blow them down in a large arc.

In order to try to overcome these difficulties Archibald made use of kites. Flax string was first employed as the flying line but, acting on the suggestion of Sir William Thompson, Archibald soon substituted steel wire. Of wire line he wrote: 'This I have found a great improvement on string. It is double the strength, one-fourth the weight, one-tenth the section, and one-half the cost.' Wire lines had been used previously, but Archibald's use of steel was to start a long period of development of techniques for flying kites by means of high-tensile steel, or 'piano-wire', as it is usually called.

Archibald's original kites were of the standard diamond type, with tails, and were made of tussore silk and bamboo. Like Alexander Wilson's kites, they were flown in tandem. At various points on the wire Archibald attached four self-recording anemometers, weighing $1\frac{1}{2}$ lb. each. With these comparatively crude tools he managed to reach heights of from 200 to 1,500 feet. Archibald himself continued work for only three years but by the 1890s his pioneering work had been followed up by the efforts of a large number of other individuals and organizations such as the

[1] Abbe writes: 'Perhaps in justice to himself the editor may remark that in July, 1876, having for the first and only time in his life a chance to spend a week on the Jersey coast, he then flew kites at Ocean Beach and Asbury Park in order to determine the depth of the sea breeze, and had the pleasure of seeing the kite which had been borne landward by the sea breeze soon reach the upper return current and be borne seaward by it.' (*Monthly Weather Review*, Vol. 24, No. 6, June 1896, p. 206.) In 1867 he had used kites to study winds under a thundercloud.

[2] Archibald, E. D., 'An Account of Some Preliminary Experiments with Biram's Anemometers Attached to Kite Strings or Wires', *Nature*, Vol. 31, No. 786, November 20, 1884, p. 66.

United States Weather Bureau, the Blue Hill Observatory near Harvard (run privately by A. Lawrence Rotch), the kite station at Trappes in France (run by Teisserenc de Bort), and the meteorological station in Breslau under Dr Weber.

Typical of the sort of work done with kites in the late nineteenth and early twentieth centuries were the researches of the U.S. Weather Bureau and the Blue Hill Observatory. Since their activities are well documented, a summary of them may serve to indicate the kind of thing being done with kites in meteorological stations at this period.

One of the earliest regular investigators was Alexander McAdie. In connexion with his studies at Harvard, he carried out experiments at Blue Hill in 1885. (Later

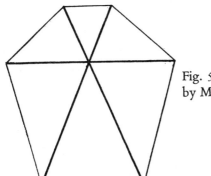

Fig. 57. Barn-door kite, as used by McAdie in 1885

he worked for the U.S. Weather Bureau.) At that time he made use of two large silk-covered kites of the common American hexagonal shape. These are sometimes known as 'barn-door' or 'house' kites (Fig. 57). They were covered in tin-foil to help collect a charge (the foil was later discovered to be unnecessary) and were flown from 1,500 feet of hemp fishing line, around which a thin copper wire was loosely wrapped. Strong charges were experienced, even in fine weather.

> It was not until August 9th [1892] that we succeeded in going through a storm with the kite still flying. About 11 a.m. the kite was sent aloft, and it remained aloft until after 10 p.m. From the observatory one can see to the west fifty or more miles, and a thunderstorm came into view just about sunset. The kite was flying steadily, and whenever a finger was held near the kite wire there was a perfect fusillade of sparks. As the darkness increased, the polished metallic and glass surfaces in the large electrometer reflected the sparks, now strong enough to jump across the air gaps, and the incessant sizzling threatened to burn out the instrument.

The vividness of the lightning in the west also made it plain that the storm was one of great violence, and as the observatory itself would be jeopardized, one of the four men present proposed to cut the wired string and let the kite go. But even that was easier said than done, for to touch the string was to receive a severe shock. It was necessary, however, to get out of the scrape, and one of the party took the kite string and broke the connection with the electrometer and insulators. While he was in the act of doing this, the others, who by this time were outside the building, saw a flash of lightning to the west of the hill. The observer who was undoing the kite wire did not see this flash. He saw a brilliant flare-up in the electrometer, and at the same instant felt a severe blow across both arms. Notwithstanding, he loosened the wire, and, dropping an end without, it took but a few moments to make it fast on the hillside some distance away from the observatory. There it remained for the rest of the night.[1]

McAdie's kites (which were, of course, of the tailed variety) were relatively unstable and would dive even when flying quite high. It was the invention, almost simultaneously, of the Eddy bow kite and the Hargrave cellular, or box, kite (described below, Chapter 8) that made practicable the regular use of kites for meteorological purposes. Eddy himself had lifted thermometers on an ordinary kite, in about 1890, but soon afterwards, having devised his bow kites and flown several of them successfully in tandem, with minimum thermometers attached, he proposed their adoption for obtaining forecasting information. Up to this time it appears that self-recording instruments had never been raised by means of kites. They were too heavy and cumbersome in the early days, but in the 1890s simple, light, and efficient self-recording instruments were built in France and were soon in use at the Blue Hill Observatory. In August 1894 Eddy brought his kites to the observatory to demonstrate their effectiveness and on August 4 made the earliest automatic record of air-temperature using kites. Five Eddy bows, having a total area of nine square metres, lifted a $2\frac{1}{4}$ lb. instrument to a height of 1,400 feet.

On various occasions during the next year, trains of Eddy kites were used at Blue Hill for raising recording instruments. In 1895–96, however, both Blue Hill and the U.S. Weather Bureau began to use the Hargrave kites which, with some modifications and improvements, continued to be employed in meteorological work for over thirty years. (The typical meteorological kite, carrying about 68 sq. ft. of supporting surface, is shown in Fig. 58.) The kite-stations were equipped with

[1] McAdie, A., 'Franklin's Kite Experiment with Modern Apparatus', *Popular Science Monthly*, Vol. 51, October 1897, pp. 739–47.

7

power-driven winches, several miles of piano-wire having a breaking-strain of about 300 lb., and clamps for attaching the trains of kites to the main line.

In 1898 the Weather Bureau had seventeen stations taking records in various parts of the country and more such stations were opened subsequently. These operations were continued until the early 1930s, but were greatly curtailed in the later years when sounding balloons were being improved.[1] After the First World War readings taken from aeroplanes superseded the kite-records, and in any case the large number of kites being flown to great heights over the country were becoming a menace to aircraft. Ellendale, the last U.S. Weather Bureau kite-station, was closed in July 1933.[2]

Modified Hargrave kites were employed on most occasions, but the Eddy kites must be given the credit for establishing a high-flying record which stood for a

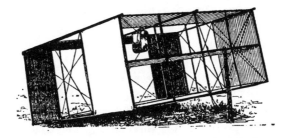

Fig. 58. Meteorological kite with meteorograph attached, *ca.* 1900–1910

number of years: on May 5, 1910, at Mount Weather, Va. (one of the Bureau's stations), a train of ten Eddy bows reached 23,385 ft. This was the highest flight recorded in the U.S., but it falls far short of the altitude of 9,740 metres (31,955 ft.) reached at Lindenberg on August 1, 1919, using a train of eight kites. This remained the world altitude record for half a century.

England lagged behind America and France in the use of kites to explore the upper atmosphere. In 1900 W. H. Dines suggested that kites be used for this purpose. The suggestion was not accepted in official circles, the lack of a suitable site for a kite-flying station being given as the reason for the refusal. In collaboration, how-ever, with another meteorologist, W. N. Shaw, Dines began a series of private kite-experiments in the summer of 1902. For this venture they were able to obtain

[1] Whitnah, D. R., *A History of the United States Weather Bureau*, Urbana, 1961, p. 103.
[2] *Ibid.*, p. 189. In some parts of the world kites continued to be used for another decade or so.

some financial support from governmental and other bodies. The first British kite-station was set up at Crinan, off the west coast of Scotland. In order to be less dependent on the strength of the wind, Dines and Shaw made use of a steam-tug to take readings at sea. (Later a naval vessel was put at their disposal.) In this way they also avoided the hazards involved in sending kite-wires over busy roads. Shortly afterwards Dines also made readings at Oxshott and Pyrton Hill.

Other kite-stations set up at this period included posts in India (1905), Egypt (1907), and one run by Teisserenc de Bort at Hald, in Jutland (1902–3). Furthermore, kite-observations were made during a number of exploring expeditions, such as the Scottish National Antarctic Expedition (1903).

Flying kites for meteorological purposes was not without its dangers. The electric potential built up on the wire was considerable at all times. The following description of its effects, by a Mr John Pyral, is quoted from the *Bradford Observer Budget:*[1]

> In 1842 and 1843 I saw kites sent up and drawn in again, and the electric shocks from them were something terrific. I have seen sparks of fire when the wire was touched with a knife blade, and men and boys severely shaken and some fall to the ground. . . . When Robert Stephenson, the great engineer, was a boy, his father bought him a donkey to ride to school, and while pursuing his journey he used to fly kites with copper wire a mile long; that is 60 years ago. . . . For fun, he used to touch the head of his donkey with the wire, and, of course, the donkey knew about it.

When repeated high flights were undertaken by the Weather Bureau, discharges frequently melted or vaporized the kite wires and sent the kites floating off, un-attached, sometimes to distances of more than twenty miles. Shocks were frequent.[2] One Weather Bureau observer reported:

> The charge coming down the kite wire rendered it incandescent and made it appear slightly larger than 1 centimeter in diameter. At the reel a cannon-like report was heard, and melted pieces of wire were scattered in every direction, liberally spraying the men on duty. None of the men was injured, although the one operating the kite reel received a slight shock. Those outside the reel house stated that the building had the appearance of being in flames. Considerable heat

---

[1] March 13, 1897.
[2] Lecornu quotes a report from *La Flandre de Dunkerque*, September 11, 1894, of a boy who was badly shaken by a bolt that struck his kite when it was flying no more than 100 yards up.

and a dazzling white glare accompanied the phenomenon. The vaporized wire left a rocket-like trail of yellowish-brown smoke which remained visible for 15 minutes throughout the entire length of the line.[1]

Potentials as high as 50,000 volts have been recorded from kites at 2,000 metres, before a discharge fused the wire. At least one fatality resulted from such discharges: in 1909 Captain Engelstad of the Swedish Navy was killed in Oslo fjord while flying a kite at about 3,000 feet. Children are now warned against flying their kites with a wire line. The warning is obviously wise.

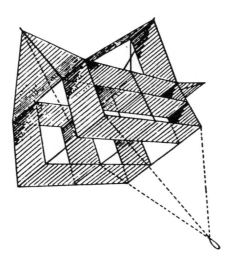

Figure 59: Compound cellular kite with wings,
late 19th—early 20th century.

[1] *Monthly Weather Review Supplement No. 11*, Washington, 1918, p. 5.

7 | Man-lifters

Kites were, of course, important precursors of the aeroplane. From the earliest times they were thought of in connexion with the flying machine, the history of their application in this field being summarized in Chapter 9. In the present context I shall concentrate on the simplest sort of flight: getting off the ground.

Just as there have been many disputes about the claims made for priority in aeroplane-flight, so there have been claims and counter-claims about the first genuine ascension in the west brought about entirely by the lifting-power of a kite. In order to try to resolve the dispute, I suggest the following criteria:

(1) The person ascending must have been an adult.
(2) The point of attachment of the kite-line at the lower end should have been stationary (that is, there must have been no ground-traction).
(3) Both the kite and its load should at some stage have risen. (That is, the kite must not have acted simply as a glider or a parachute.)
(4) In view of the possibility of rapid fluctuation of wind-speed it is probably unnecessary to apply any criterion of height or of duration.

If these criteria are accepted, it will be seen that some of the so-called flights, though interesting in themselves, are disqualified.

The first mention of a western man-lifter appears to be a brief passage in the Kircher book already referred to. He points out on p. 827 that a kite may lift a man if he pulls correctly on the line. No details are given concerning any occasion on which a man actually flew, and I think we may dismiss Kircher's comment as speculation.

The first specific western claim that I know of is one reported by Lecornu.[1] He

[1] Lecornu, J., *Les Cerfs-volants*, Paris, 1902, p. 124.

mentions a newspaper story of a flight by an English woman in the late eighteenth century. His quoted reference is, however, corrupt, and I have been unable to obtain any further confirmation. It seems likely that the story is apocryphal.

The first documented account of a flight which may qualify according to my criteria is that organized by George Pocock, whose famous *char-volant* is discussed in Chapter 10. Pocock was a schoolteacher in Bristol. He was first heard of in 1795, when he was in charge of a boarding school on St. Michael's Hill. Five years later he opened an academy in Prospect Avenue which continued to function until some years after his death in 1843. Pocock, who had been interested in kites for many years, published, in 1827, a curious little book about kite-drawn carriages. The style is very pedantic, but the facts are clearly stated. The following is from the second edition, published posthumously (and anonymously) in 1851:

> These buoyant sails, possessing immense power, will, as we have before remarked, serve for floating observatories. . . . Elevated in the air, a single sentinel, with a prospective, could watch and report the advance of the most powerful forces while yet at a great distance; he could mark their line of march, the composition of their force, and their general strength, long before he could be seen by the enemy.
> . . . Nor was less progress made in the experimental department, when large weights were required to be raised or transposed. While on this subject, we must not omit to observe, that the first person who soared aloft in the air, by this invention, was a lady, whose courage would not be denied this test of its strength. An arm chair was brought on the ground; then, lowering the cordage of the Kite, by slackening the lower brace, the chair was firmly lashed to the main line, and the lady took her seat. The main-brace being hauled taut, the huge Buoyant Sail rose aloft with its fair burden, continuing to ascend to the height of one hundred yards. On descending, she expressed herself much pleased at the easy motion of the Kite, and the delightful prospect she had enjoyed. Soon after this, another experiment of a similar nature took place, when the inventor's son successfully carried out a design not less safe than bold– that of scaling, by this powerful ærial machine, the brow of a cliff, two hundred feet in perpendicular height. Here, after safely landing, he again took his seat in a chair expressly prepared for the purpose, and, detaching the swivel-line which kept it at its elevation, glided gently down the cordage to the hand of the director. The Buoyant Sail employed on this occasion was thirty feet in height, with a proportionate spread of canvas. The rise of this machine was most majestic, and nothing could surpass the steadiness with which it was manœuvred, the certainty with which it answered the action of the braces, and the ease with which its power was lessened or increased . . . Subsequently to this, an experiment of a very bold and novel character was made upon an extensive

down, where a large waggon with a considerable load was drawn along, whilst this huge machine at the same time carried an observer aloft in the air, realising almost the romance of flying.[1]

(The young lady mentioned in this quotation was in fact Pocock's daughter, Martha.) The date of these flights is unclear, but they seem to have taken place about 1825. If Pocock's children were then of adult stature,[2] this may qualify as the first genuine man-carrying kite in the west.

The next claim is a little-known one by a Frenchman. Although it does not meet my criteria, since the ascender was only a child at the time, it is of interest in that the kite used was simply an enormously scaled-up version of the conventional 'pear' kite. (See Fig. 54.) The following is a translation of a letter about the flight which appeared in *Le Cerf-volant*:

> I read with interest your article on man-carrying kites, but I found no mention of Dr Jules Laval of Dijon who, in 1854, made several experiments with a kite at least 10 metres high by 6 wide, flown by four or five men. At the end of its tail it carried a little wickerwork chair, in which he got me to sit, holding on to me by means of a rope. At this time the kite was some 50 metres in the air.
>
> The men were finding it very difficult to hold the kite down and as they were getting rather near to the Suzon river they tied the line to an elder log which was lying behind a milestone at a turning in the road. Friction caused by the tension on the line caused the log to catch fire and the cord broke. I fell from a height of 9 or 10 metres, but quite slowly and was not injured.
>
> We returned home, and I have never again flown from a kite.
>
> – H. Lieutet
>
> N.B. I was born at Dijon, on June 18, 1843. I was thus eleven years old. I was already very tall. Today I measure nearly six feet, but I no longer remember how heavy I then was.[3]

At this point mention may be made of a kite-flight arranged by Colladon, whose electric kites were discussed in the previous chapter. Though in no sense a manned

---

[1] [Pocock, G.] *A Treatise of the Aeropleustic Art*, London, 1851, pp. 19–20, 53–4.

[2] It is difficult to be certain about this. Martha (who later became the mother of W. G. Grace) was born in 1812. She was therefore only 13 in 1825, but the flight may have taken place somewhat later. As Pocock's sons were older than Martha, the flight to the cliff may also qualify. For facts about Pocock and his family, I am grateful to Miss E. Ralph, City Archivist, Bristol Archives Office.

[3] *Le Cerf-volant*, Vol. 2, No. 11, June 1910, p. 158.

flight, this provides an amusing interlude. In the summer of 1844 Colladon had been experimenting with self-releasing 'messengers' which travelled up the line of the kite and then dropped a parachute when they struck the kite's bridle. He decided to try sending up a full-sized dummy which was accordingly made, complete with umbrella, boots, and chair (Fig. 60). Although the dummy weighed 15 lb. it rose to a distance of about 200 yards, much to the amazement of the populace. A coach-load of people who arrived on the scene as the placid dummy was rising thought they were witnessing the feat of a very courageous young man.

In 1857 J.-M. Le Bris, whose bird-shaped glider has become quite famous in the

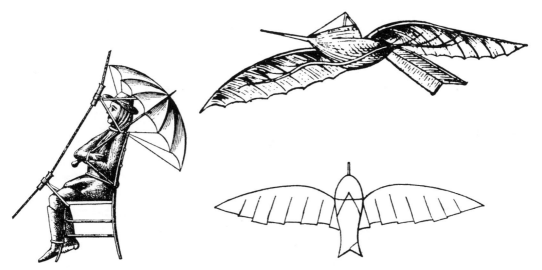

Fig. 60. Colladon's ascending dummy, 1844   Fig. 61. Le Bris's bird-form gliders

history of manned flight, made an ascension in which his glider functioned as a kite, though the lift was produced partly by horse-traction. The bird (Fig. 61) was mounted on a carriage and pulled against the wind by the horse, while Le Bris controlled the machine from inside the nacelle. The glider rose and should have been released, to make its own way to earth under Le Bris's guidance. Unfortunately the cord caught on the carriage and the horse bolted. The cord thereupon broke free, wrapped itself around the body of the coachman and lifted him into the air also. Le Bris's glider had in fact acted as a two-man-lifter.

All the flights so far considered were of a more or less casual variety, but in 1859 an Irish priest, Fr. E. J. Cordner, designed a system of multiple hexagon kites for lifting people to land in case of shipwreck. As this is the first time kites had been designed specifically as man-lifters, Cordner's system is of some importance. The following description is quoted from the patent specification (dated 1860):

> . . . I prefer carrying my Invention into effect by employing kites constructed so as to fly and produce their effect without tails or other like appendages, the string or line of the first or uppermost kite being attached to the adjacent kite, and the string or line of this to that next adjacent, and so on throughout a series of as many kites as may be required for any particular purpose . . . The primary object which I have in view is that of raising and transporting to the shore by these means a light car or basket from a stranded vessel on a lee shore. In a car or basket one person or even several persons might be conveyed safely to land, and by suitably arranging the kites, cars, and their appendages, and furnishing them with hauling lines and other appliances, a continuous communication may be established with the shore for the safe landing of persons and property. The operation will be as follows:– When a vessel has struck, which in almost every case is on a lee shore, a common size kite is elevated in the usual way on board the ship. When a sufficient quantity of cord is veered out to enable the kite to remain suspended in the atmosphere, the end of the cord on board is attached in a peculiar manner to the back of another and larger kite, this second kite is then suffered to ascend, and the end of its suspending rope is attached in a similar manner to the back of a third and still larger kite, and this process is repeated till any amount of elevating and tractive power has been obtained, the size of each succeeding kite being limited by convenience. When a sufficient power of elevation and traction has been attained, a light boat of basketwork or other material, capable of containing one or more persons, is attached to the suspending rope of the last kite, more rope is then veered away and the light boat with its cargo will eventually reach the land without any chance of its being submerged in the sea, no matter how great may be the elevation of the waves. The boat is suspended from the kite line by a pulley or block in the bow, and another in the stern, and when it has reached the shore the person it contains descends, and retaining in his hands a light rope attached to the bow he suffers the boat gradually to return to the ship, which it will be sure to do in consequence of the elevation of the kite line from the diminished weight which it has to support, but which result is also secured by a rope attached to the stern of the boat, the end of which has been retained by those on board the shipwrecked vessel, and can be hauled on by them when necessary. . . The kites are generally of a hexagonal shape covered with calico, linen, or other material, and are so constructed as to pack into convenient sized boxes.

It is not known whether this system was ever used in connexion with a shipwreck, but George Wenham told Octave Chanute that the Cordner system had been 'tested by transporting a number of persons purposely assembled on a rock off the Irish coast, one at a time, through the air to the main land, quite above the waves, and it was claimed that the invention of thus superposing kites so as to obtain great tractive power was applicable to various other purposes, such as towing vessels, etc.' Further documentation seems to be lacking, but here again we have a genuine case of a man-lifter, provided that Wenham, usually a reliable reporter, has given us, through Chanute, an accurate account.[1]

From the middle of the century on, with the increasing interest in the possibilities of free flight, attempts at manned kite flight grew in number and seriousness. The

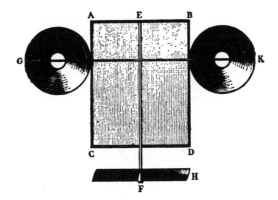

Fig. 62. Biot's cone-kite with stabilizing screw, 1880

French experimenter Biot, who designed the kite in Fig. 62, consisting of a rectangular plane with twin wind-cones on each side and a stabilizing screw at the bottom, claimed to have flown from a kite in 1868. What is known of Biot reveals him as a most ingenious experimenter, but I have been able to discover no further details concerning his flight.

An English balloonist named Joseph Simmons, who seems to have been something of a charlatan, claimed to have made ascents from a huge man-lifter in 1876. When the experiment was repeated in Brussels, however, on Sunday, October 8, 1876, Simmons failed completely. His apparatus was imposing in its size. Sometimes only one kite was used, but the system was designed to make use of two if necessary. The first of these, the 'pilot kite', was a cloth square almost 50 feet by 50. This was fixed to a pair of diagonal rods tied at their centres. The cloth was to fill out

[1] For the work of Wenham and Chanute, see the Bibliography.

so as to present a concave surface to the wind. This kite, already very large, was to be used to raise a second and even larger one. Below the kites a nacelle was suspended. Simmons's intention, at the Brussels experiment, was to launch the kite (using the services of ten assistants), seat himself in the nacelle, and then rise some two or three hundred yards. At that point he would order the kite to be released and, manipulating a system of guy ropes to adjust the attitude and centre of gravity, would allow the nacelle to glide gently to earth. The kite, however, kept falling to

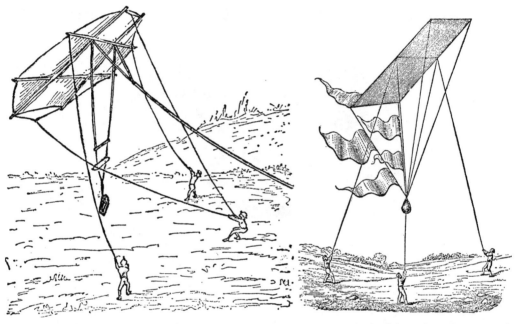

Fig. 63. Maillot's man-lifter, 1885–6   Fig. 64. Weight-lifting kite from South America, *ca.* 1870

the ground after rising thirty feet or so, and the attempt was finally abandoned. The account in *l'Aéronaute*[1] describes Simmons calmly smoking a cigarette during the launching attempts and afterwards phlegmatically folding the equipment, with a comment that the wind had been insufficient. It seems more likely that his unstable apparatus was to blame.

Simmons is hardly to be taken seriously as a manned-kite flier, but a Frenchman

[1] Vol. 9, No. 11, November 1876, pp. 313–4. A theoretical anticipation of Simmons appeared in *Le Magasin Pittoresque*, Vol. 12, No. 21, 1844, p. 166.

from the same period, Maillot (*b.* 1844), was an experimenter of some calibre. While a prisoner in Germany at the time of the Franco-Prussian War, he became interested in the possibilities of kite-flight as a replacement for balloons. Later, between 1884 and 1886, he carried out a series of tests with kites of man-lifting proportions. Maillot never flew from his kites, having been dissuaded from the attempt by friends, but he raised ballast as heavy as a man and must be credited with having built a kite capable of acting consistently as a man-lifter, though it was so clumsy a piece of apparatus as to be virtually useless. The great octagonal kite illustrated in Fig. 63 had a surface area of 72 square metres and weighed 165 lb. It is possible that Maillot

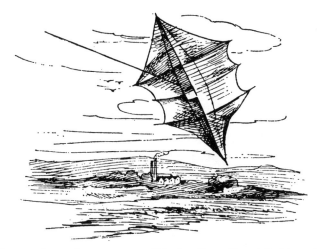

Fig. 65. General appearance of Baden-Powell's 36-ft. kite, 1894

(though perhaps indebted to Birt – see pp. 106-7) found the basic idea for the man-lifter in an article published in *Le Magasin Pittoresque* in 1873, which includes the illustration reproduced here as Fig. 64, showing a large kite which was noticed in South America. It is not suggested that the kite was used as a man-lifter, but like Maillot's it lifted ballast of some weight.[1]

It was intended that the flier of Maillot's kite should be able to vary the angle of incidence and the lateral disposition by pulling on the guy ropes. Since in the event only ballast was raised, these manipulations were carried out by men on the ground. Although Maillot did not ascend in his kite, he seems to have regretted

[1] *L'Aéronaute*, Vol. 19, No. 7, July 1886, pp. 134–8; *Le Magasin Pittoresque*, Vol. 40, 1873, p. 280.

taking the advice of his friends. In later years (even as late as 1909), rather lonely and lacking funds, he continued to experiment and plan for an ascent, but he died without achieving his goal.

Among other inventions produced by Maillot was a moderately successful system of anti-lightning kites. Early in this century he also made a little money by marketing a special form of winged box kite which, in 1905, won a prize at the *Concours de cerfs-volants de la Société française de navigation aérienne*.[1]

Captain B. F. S. Baden-Powell, of the Scots Guards,[2] said that he remembered once sending a grasshopper up on a kite when he was a boy and that he decided to try to do the same for a man. He succeeded in his aim, constructing what was to be the first generally reliable system of man-lifters. Unlike so many other kite-experiments, Baden-Powell's were always well documented. The first ascent took place on June 27, 1894, at Pirbright Camp, using a kite 36 ft. high. This was approximately hexagonal in shape, had a surface area of about 500 square feet, and was made of cambric stretched over a framework of bamboo. The kite was flown from two lines below which a basket was suspended. Men were several times raised to a height of about 10 ft. with this apparatus, but as it was not considered very safe, higher ascents were never attempted. Experiments with the kite continued almost daily for several weeks, during which time many men were successfully lifted.

Although a kite of this size was clearly impracticable, Baden-Powell had made the important advance of getting it to fly without a tail. Under the pressure of the wind the kite bent back from side to side, so producing a natural dihedral which made it stable. The practical successor of this giant was a tandem arrangement of a number of small kites, each of about 110 square feet in area. During the autumn of 1895 he several times lifted men, using from four to seven of the kites, depending on the strength of the wind. The new design was a simple hexagon, which bowed in the wind as before (Fig. 66). Baden-Powell patented this design, which he called the 'levitor' kite. In September 1895 he exhibited the system before the British Association, when he and others were lifted to a height of 100 feet, this being the length of the rope by which the car was hauled down.

Baden-Powell's military profession was to prove of some importance in the development of the kite. He proposed its adoption by the army, to create observation

[1] *Le Cerf-volant*, Vol. 1, No. 4, November 1909, p. 48.

[2] Brother of the Chief Scout, editor of *The Aeronautical Journal*, and later President of the Aeronautical Society.

posts from which a man could watch enemy lines (which, he said, gave a general the same opportunities as he might gain by having a peep at his opponent's hand at whist). Baden-Powell's kites were never officially adopted, but the suggestion itself bore fruit later when Cody developed his variation of the box kite (see below, pp. 160-2). For a few years, until the development of the aeroplane made kites redundant, the army had a small 'kite corps'.

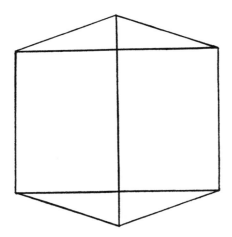

Fig. 66. Baden-Powell's 12-ft. patent 'levitor' kite, 1895

Baden-Powell found his kites hard work on occasions. In an article called 'War Kites'[1] he relates some incidents:

When I got an . . . opportunity, I fixed a kite directly on to a horse. This did very well for one kite, but that wasn't enough to lift a man, so one day we arranged about half-a-dozen kites in tandem, laid them on the ground, fixed the car in place, and set out a rope about 1,000 ft. long, and attached the far end of this to the horse. In order to get the desired space, this rope was carried over an oak fence. A groom was to ride the horse, and look out for the signal to start.

Well, all was ready, the signal given, and off went the horse. Just as the kites were going to lift, I noticed something not quite right with one of them. I shouted to stop the horse, but the groom didn't hear. I ran forward to set the kite right if possible, but I only pulled it over, so that it turned turtle and scraped along the ground. The other kites followed suit. I yelled out to stop the horse, but he, finding something extraordinary pulling behind, became frightened and bolted!

There was a nice show! The horse tearing as hard as he could go across the

[1] *The Aeronautical Journal*, Vol. 3, No. 1, January 1899, pp. 1-6.

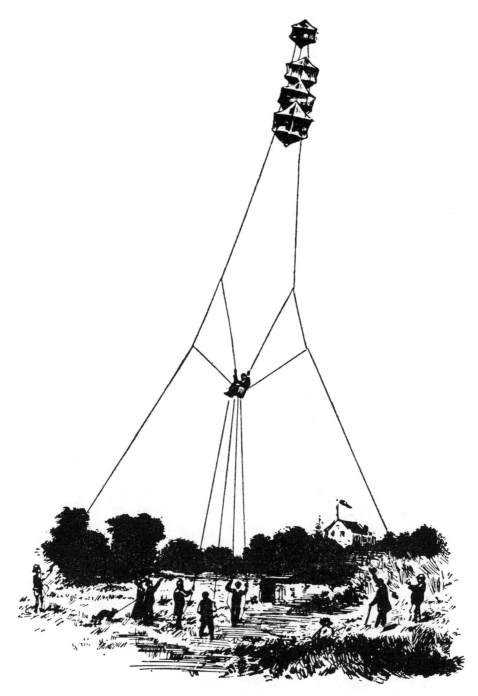

Fig. 67. Ascent with four 'levitor' kites

field, the car dragging and bumping along the ground, the kites floundering along, continually catching in the ground and breaking their frames. But soon the car came to the fence. There was a crash and a bang, some yards of fencing were hurled to the ground, but the horse thus suddenly checked, turned a somersault, and threw its rider like an arrow from a bow. But they came up smiling.

Another day I very nearly experienced a new sensation. There was a set of kites flying low. A long light line was hanging from the cable, and the greater part of this was lying entangled in the ground. I was busy trying to get it disentangled when, for some reason, the kites suddenly took it into their heads to rise. The cord rushed through my hands, the entanglement about my feet suddenly

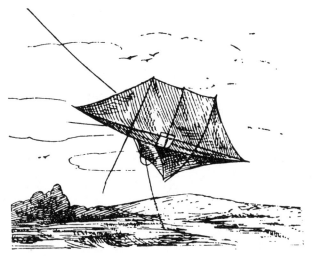

Fig. 68. An accident which once occurred to Baden-Powell's 36-ft. kite
(Drawing from a contemporary photograph)

closed tightly round my ankle, up went the kites, up went my foot, down I went on my back, dragged along thus for some yards, and was just about to be lifted up a few hundred feet by my ankle, when a gallant bystander rushed up and held me while we rapidly got out a knife and cut the cord.

Shortly after Baden-Powell's first experiments, Lawrence Hargrave (who had not heard of Baden-Powell's success) managed to raise himself by means of a train of four of his cellular kites. With his usual meticulousness, Hargrave describes his ascent, which took place on November 12, 1894:

The sling seat was toggled on and the writer got aboard with a hand anemometer and a clinometer. . . . In about a quarter of an hour the wind freshened and raised the experimenter, when he found the velocity of the wind to be 18.6 miles per hour, the spring balance reading one hundred and eighty pounds maximum. The wind falling lighter, kites and experimenter came down. Several more ascents were made, but not of sufficient duration to read the anemometer . . . However, a long and strong puff eventually came and sent everything up like a shot. A careful reading showed the wind velocity to be twenty-one miles per hour, with two hundred and forty pounds maximum pull on the spring balance, the total weight aloft being two hundred and eight pounds five ounces. . . . The descent in every case was of the gentlest description. . . . The kite line used is common Manilla clothes line, and is not easy to handle when strained.[1]

Hargrave rose to only sixteen feet but, as he pointed out, 'the conditions would be identical if the kites had been held by a mile of piano wire instead of the clothes line'.

One further ascent from this period may be mentioned. On January 19, 1896, Lieutenant H. D. Wise, of the U.S. Army, raised himself by means of a train of four Hargrave kites. In 1932 he wrote an amusing account of his youthful experiments:

Having built some very large kites, with nearly 200 square feet of lifting surface, and having obtained rope and a large winch from the post quartermaster, we were soon ready to send aloft a man for the first kite ascent. This man was 'Jimmy', by which name we designated an old uniform stuffed and weighted to 150 pounds.

Three kites were sent up in tandem and, where the cord of the second joined the main line, 'Jimmy', in a boatswain's chair, was tied on. The third kite was attached a little below that point. A blustery veering wind was blowing, so before Jimmy left the ground he took a severe mauling. Finally, however, he rose and floated gracefully out above New York Harbor some 200 feet above the water.

Ferry boats were nearly capsized by Jimmy's admirers who crowded their rails and whistles shrieked hurrah to his unhearing ears. . . . The next day the same tandem was put up but, profiting by the mauling Jimmy had received on his first trip, a different method was used for the 'take-off'. At the junction of the cords of the two upper kites a pulley was rove to the main line and over it passed a hundred foot halyard to one end of which was fastened the boatswain's chair. When the pulley had risen about 50 feet, Jimmy was hoisted, the halyard secured to the main line and the kites were run out.

Jimmy, however, was due for more trouble. The second kite, taking a dive, fouled the main line and collapsed. The jerk on the upper kite tore out its center

[1] Hargrave, L., 'Paper on Aeronautical Work', *Journal and Proceedings of the Royal Society of New South Wales*, Vol. 29, 1895, pp. 46–7.

rib and Jimmy, followed by the one remaining kite, plunged to the ground where, unlike Humpty Dumpty, his pieces were gathered together again.

Profiting by this accident, we arranged the tandem differently. The center ribs of two kites were bound together. Two tandems, each of two kites, were made. The upper or smaller kite of each of these was attached to the back of the lower which it thus steadied. Where the two tandem cords were brought together the pulley was rove in and the single cord from that point was supported where necessary by other kites.

A day or so after we had made this new arrangement, and when there was a brisk breeze blowing, I took my seat in the boatswain's chair and was hoisted to

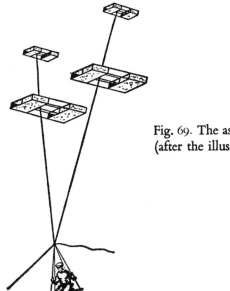

Fig. 69. The ascent of Wise's 'Jimmy', 1896 (after the illustration in his own article)

the pulley where I secured the halyard. I then signaled to have the kites run out and had the thrill of feeling myself borne smoothly and steadily upward . . . Ferry boat passengers were apparently as interested in me as they had been in Jimmy and the whistles gave me the same vociferous greeting. It would be an interesting question of law as to how much the responsibility might have been mine had one of those ferry boats capsized but it is certain that no damages could have been collected because all of my assets had gone to the construction of the apparatus.

The daily papers had quite fully exploited these recent experiments so my mail was more than ever full of letters with just the necessary suggestions and advice. One man even sent me a parachute for, having read of my 'miraculous escape', supposing it was I who fell when Jimmy got his tumble, he thought I should guard against such accidents.[1]

Before Wise was successful he suffered some startling accidents:

The same kites that bore the dummy aloft had been sent up about two hundred feet, when the two men who were assisting me went for another kite, leaving me alone at the windlass. Noticing that the rope was in danger of being cut by the cogs, I put on the brake, and passing around to the front, bore down on the rope, which did not appear to be under great strain. In order to readjust the rope on the drum it was necessary to relieve the tension. Near the windlass a piece of rope had been spliced to the main line as a leader for the cord of another kite. This I wrapped

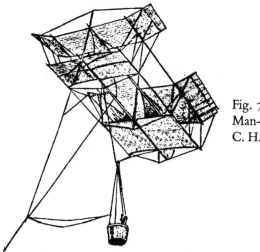

Fig. 70.
Man-lifter designed by
C. H. Lamson, *ca.* 1897

around my waist and tied with a bow; then, drawing my knife, I cut the main line from the windlass. I was not long in discovering my mistake, for as the rope parted the knife flew from my hand, I was jerked over on my back, and started for a sleigh-ride across the grass at a rapid pace. In my effort to untie the bow, I pulled the wrong end and made a hard knot. Finally I managed to get to my feet; but this was little better, and in spite of my efforts I was rapidly approaching the sea-wall. Where it would all have ended I am unable to say; but I am inclined to believe that I should have needed no ferry ticket to Staten Island had not a friendly lamp-

[1] Wise, H. D., 'Flying in the Beginning', *Scientific American*, Vol. 147, September 1932, pp. 212–3.

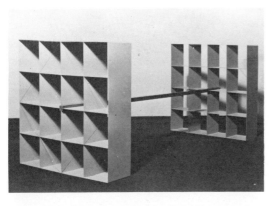

41. Reproduction of the original Hargrave box kite, made of tinplate, 1893.

42. A later Hargrave box kite, with fin, 1898.

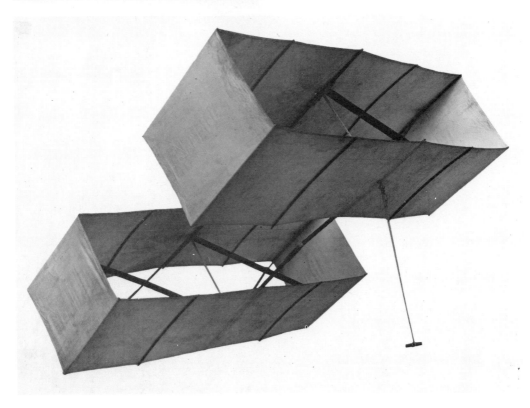

43. The fully developed Hargrave box kite.

44. Hargrave with a three-cell box kite, developed so that the line attachment could be near the centre, January 19, 1908.

45. Hargrave with a single-cell box kite, 1909.

46. Two of Hargrave's soaring kites, with Stanwell Park in the background, May 1898.

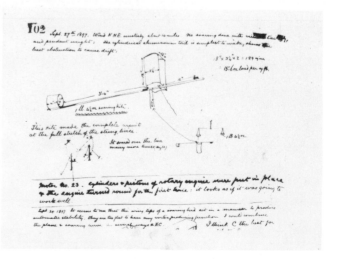

47. Part of a page from Hargrave's notebooks. Somewhat reduced.

48. Meteorological box kite, as used at Blue Hill. *Smithsonian Institution*

49. Launching a meteorological box kite. *Smithsonian Institution*

50. Landing a meteorological box kite by the 'underrunning' method. *Smithsonian Institution*

51. Kite-glider designed by S. F. Cody, 1905, showing below-wing ailerons.

52. Cody man-lifter kite.

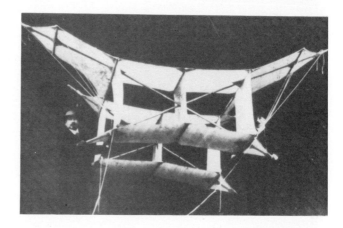

53. Cody with one of his man-lifters.

54, 55. Cody man-lifters at Whale Island, May 1903.

56. Lamson's biplane 'aero-curve' kite, 1897.

57. Triplane version of Lamson's 'aerocurve' kite, *ca.* 1897. *Smithsonian Institution*

58. Kite-flying at St Louis Exhibit, 1904.

59. Herring–Beeson keel kite, with adjustable elevator-plane. *Smithsonian Institution*

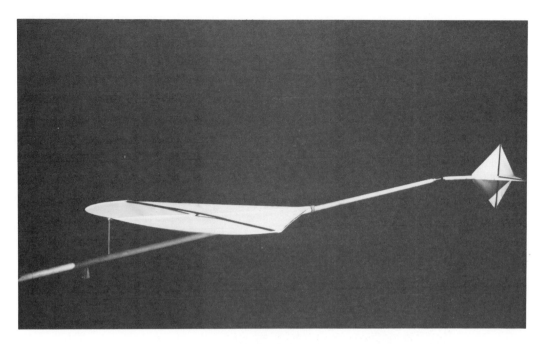

60. Reproduction of Cayley's kite-glider, 1804. *Crown Copyright, Science Museum, London*

61. Gallaudet laterally controlled kite-glider. Wing-warping experiment of 1898. *Smithsonian Institution*

62. Wright brothers' No. 1 glider flown as a kite, 1900.

63. Wilbur Wright (right) with a bird kite. *Smithsonian Institution*

64. Voisin-Archdeacon float-glider on the Seine, 1905.

post happened to be directly in the line of travel. I approached it with outstretched arms, clasped it in a fond embrace, and there I hung until assistance arrived.[1]

After these three successful attempts on three continents, kite-ascents became increasingly common. Various systems were developed, probably the most spectacular being those of Cody (see below, pp. 160-2), and the giant tetrahedrals of Alexander Graham Bell (see pp. 154-9).

In all the man-lifting instances so far quoted, the flier was suspended some way *below* his kite. It was not until June 19, 1897, that the first ascent was made either in, or very close to, the kite itself, so using the kite as a true manned vehicle. This was the ascent of one of the greatest of all kite-designers, Charles H. Lamson, the form of whose kites is discussed in the following chapter. Near Portland, Maine, he rose to some 50 feet, holding on directly to one of his 'aero-curve' kites.[2] As the kite was launched by helpers, he ran with it until it was airborne, after which he was really piloting a captive aeroplane.

Fig. 71. The flight of Colladon's dummy, 1844.

---

[1] Wise, H. D., 'Experiments with Kites', *The Century Illustrated Monthly Magazine*, Vol. 54, No. 1, May 1897, p. 84.

[2] Varney, G. J., 'Kite-Flying in 1897', *Popular Science Monthly*, Vol. 53, No. 1, May 1898, pp. 48-63.

8 | The Development of the Form of the Kite

In Asia and the Pacific, as I have indicated, kites of a multitude of shapes have been used for centuries. Most of them are tailless and many are of very sophisticated design. (Some Chinese bird-kites, for instance, have independently controllable wings, manipulated by twin lines.) The following is an attempt to provide a rough classification of the kite-forms used in that part of the world:

(1) Fighting-kites: (*a*) rectangular, as in Korea; (*b*) flown on a diagonal, as in the ubiquitous Nagasaki kite and its variants.
(2) Fishing-kites: leaf-shaped or compounded from leaves. Indonesia, Melanesia, and the west Pacific.
(3) Figure-kites for ceremonial or display purposes. Asia and the Pacific generally.
(4) Other geometric forms, either simple or complex, such as the various Malayan humming kites, the Japanese *wan–wan*, etc.
(5) Children's kites, usually of simple geometric shape, and often stabilized by tails.
(6) 'Three-dimensional kites'. Kites of simple biplane construction are known in the Malayan area; there has also been some suggestion that the box kite was in use in the east before its invention by Hargrave, but I have not been able to confirm this.

In the west, by contrast, kites remained quite crude in design until late in the nineteenth century.

In discussing the development of the design of western kites one must be fully aware of the various aims of kite-constructors. The child normally has only one aim:

to make his kite fly as high as possible, and with reasonable stability. But kites may intentionally be made to fly low, or to fly unstably. The following are the most important demands that may be made of a kite:

(1) *Stability.* The kite should rapidly find a position of equilibrium and should resist changes of position due to sudden fluctuations in the weather conditions. Stability is obviously desirable for any purposes which require the kite to act as a centre of observation, such as in kite-photography, meteorological work, or military look-outs.

(2) *Manœuvrability (low stability).* Stability is a disadvantage in a kite which is to be used to move out of the line of the wind, as for kite-fighting. For such purposes as life-saving, a kite needs to be conditionally stable – that is, it must be manœuvrable and capable of responding to changes of tension on the guiding lines, but must retain any new direction imparted to it.

(3) *Efficiency.* A kite is said to be efficient if it has a high ratio of lift to drag, that is, if it rises to a high angle with the horizon. Maximum efficiency is needed if a kite is to be used to fly to great heights, as in making observations of the upper atmosphere.

(4) *High drag (low efficiency).* It may be desirable to have a kite which will fly stably, but will remain at a low angle to the horizon. This is the case when a kite is to be used to provide traction – e.g., of a boat, a life-line, etc., – or to carry lines across rivers and gorges.

(5) *Suitability for the conditions.* A kite must be designed to cope with the weather conditions in which it must fly. A heavy kite will not fly in a light breeze, but a light-weather model may prove either unstable or too fragile in a gale. The U.S. Weather Bureau made kites that could fly through rain-squalls, and kites have been flown during snow-storms.

It was the first of these criteria that occupied designers in the early days. Until fairly recently, European kites were never markedly stable. Before the late nineteenth century the bow and box kites were unknown and only the inherently unstable flat kites, discussed in Chapter 4, were used. Although these are called flat kites they do not in fact lie perfectly flat in flight: if they did, they would be almost uncontrollable. The cover billows out to form concave pockets behind the frame, so helping the kite to achieve some degree of stability. No intentional curvature was introduced, however, and no keel was provided; these kites all needed, therefore, to be provided with tails.

Although such kites were the standard, many variations on the basic pattern were devised. Books of the nineteenth century in particular show plane-surface kites of a great variety of outline: clowns, animals, birds, dancing girls, etc. As the bird and the sailor in Fig. 72 reveal, most such figures can be produced using a modified diamond or arch-top frame. Bird-kites have always been especially popular. It is reported that when Napoleon III was reviewing troops after being named President in 1848, someone flew over his head a kite in the shape of an eagle–politically a rather rash act, of course. (In response to an indignant order, the kite was quickly cut down.)[1]

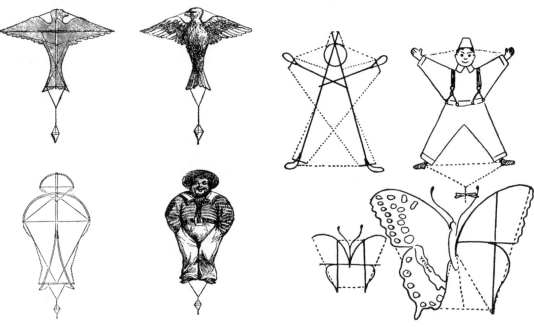

Fig. 72. Bird and sailor kites. Variations of the diamond and arch-top

Fig. 73. Boy and butterfly kites. Variations on the 'barn-door' design

As discussed above, Franklin made use of a diamond kite, but by the nineteenth century the standard American child's kite seems to have been the irregular but symmetrical hexagon illustrated in the 'barn-door' kite (Fig. 57). The origin of this design is unclear but ornamental variations of it soon became very numerous. The boy and butterfly kites in Fig. 73 were very popular early in the twentieth century.

The three-stick hexagon is the kite used by the Franklin Kite Club, by Abbe in

[1] Lecornu, J., *Les Cerfs-volants*, Paris, 1902, pp. 213–4.

1876, and by William A. Eddy before he developed his famous bow kite. Eddy reported that his first experiment with a hexagon kite was undertaken in 1865 when, as a boy, he tried to raise a lantern on a kite tail. The lantern was soon extinguished by the motion of the kite and in later years Eddy realized that he would have been more successful if he had tied the lantern to the towing point (the point at which the line meets the kite's bridle). His serious adult interest in kites began in 1887, when he learned of the experiments of Woodbridge Davis, who devised a manœuvrable life-saving kite (see below, p. 171). Eddy experimented with methods of flying in train (flying several kites on the one line) and, on May 9, 1891, succeeded in

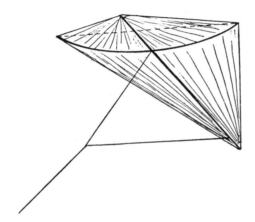

Fig. 74. Structure of Eddy's bow kite, 1891–2

raising a train of five hexagon kites (with tails) to an estimated 4,000–6,000 feet. As the tailed kites proved troublesome, however, especially for flying in train, Eddy set about designing a tailless variety. His results constituted the first genuine advance in western kite-design since the development of the diamond shape in Renaissance times.

Eddy had heard of the buoyant Javanese kite before 1890, but, being unable to obtain measurements, had to re-invent it for himself. In 1893 he saw one of the native Javanese kites in the Javanese Village at the Columbian Exposition and found that his own kite was very similar in principle. Subsequently some improvements were incorporated at the suggestion of a friend who had made and flown such kites in Cape Town, where they had apparently been imported from the Malayan area.

Eddy, who was interested in using kites for meteorology, for photography, and for other purposes requiring steady lift to great heights, wanted to develop kites with improved stability and efficiency. In this he was remarkably successful. The Eddy bow kite (or Malay kite, as it is sometimes called) has many advantages over the diamond and hexagon kites that had been used hitherto (Fig. 74). It is self-stabilizing both fore-and-aft and laterally. Stability in the fore-and-aft direction is assured by the prominent 'brow' formed by the cross stick. Pitching of the kite in one direction is automatically compensated by an increased pressure on either top or bottom sections, tending to correct the movement. Lateral stability is secured by the 'keel' formed by the spine. The kite-cover, lying back from the keel, functions like the sides of a boat, keeping the kite evenly trimmed. Because of this stability no tail is needed. Efficiency is also good because of the comparatively low weight per unit area, and because the kite is wider than most earlier designs. Better lift is provided by a short, wide kite than by a long narrow one. In addition, the natural curve of the cover over the bottom part of the kite tends to act somewhat like a cambered aerofoil when the kite is flying near the horizontal. (A Malay kite will, in fact, act as a good glider if ballasted and propelled horizontally, free of its string.)

The importance of Eddy's work lay in his making the bow kite widely known among experimenters. As I have pointed out, bow kites of various sorts had been used for centuries in the east, and had often been introduced, in small numbers, into the west. Furthermore, Eddy was not, strictly speaking, the first western designer to use the bow in conjunction with the lozenge configuration. A kite strikingly like Eddy's was described in *La Nature* in 1887, but, unlike Eddy's widely publicized design, it seems to have had virtually no impact on other experimenters.

Eddy had some amusing stories to tell about his early experiments with his new kites. Spectators were not only astonished to see a grown man with bushy moustaches and derby hat flying large kites, but they jeered at his attempts to do the impossible: fly a kite without a tail. One little boy approached him one day and said: 'My papa . . . I heard him say one day that you ought to have a keeper. What did he mean by that?' The jeering took a slightly more serious turn when one of Eddy's friends became enthusiastic for the new kites and began to fly them from his roof. The friend, who was a doctor, soon found that he had to abandon his pastime when his patients started to patronize a saner practitioner.

Eddy experimented with a very large number of kites in train, flying as many as eighteen from the one line. A result of this was the relatively frequent incidence of break-aways. On one occasion a train of eight broke away and went careering across Staten Island to New York Bay, trailing its line over lawns and housetops, to the amazement of hundreds of people. After two kites had come down, the remaining six were caught on a telegraph line, from which Eddy rescued them after having given chase first on a ferry and then by train.

On another occasion two kites broke away and started out to sea. The dangling line passed over a moored coal barge on which a man was working. Feeling something tickle his neck he put up his hand and grasped the kite-line, very surprised at what he had caught. Eddy had some trouble in persuading the bargee to give up his prize.[1]

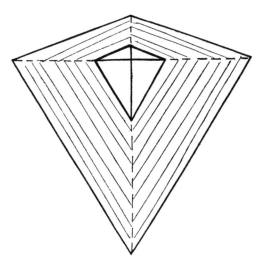

Fig. 75. Eddy's perforated kite, 1892

Kite breakaways were not uncommon among meteorologists. The great French meteorologist Teisserenc de Bort had several thrilling experiences with breakaway wire lines which trailed across Paris, being caught in power lines and in railway locomotives. On one occasion a kite which was being flown in Calais broke away and did not come to ground until it had reached Kent.[2] Even more remarkable was the journey of a pair of German kites flying at a height of $2\frac{1}{2}$ miles over Berlin and

[1] Moffett, C., 'Scientific Kite Flying', *McClure's Magazine*, Vol. 6, No. 4, March 1896, pp. 379–92.
[2] 'The Descent of a French Balloon and Kite in England', *The Aeronautical Journal*, Vol. 4, No. 3, July 1900, pp. 139–40.

carrying self-recording instruments. They broke away, bearing two miles of wire with them, and did not fall until they were nearly 100 miles from their starting point.[1]

Eddy was a keen photographer and did much to develop the technique of photography from kites. He also suggested and helped to perfect many other applications of kites for both civil and military purposes, but he made only one other contribution to the development of the kite itself. In 1892 he read that some Chinamen in Washington, D.C., were in the habit of flying kites in which small holes had been cut to steady their movement. Eddy experimented with perforated covers in an attempt to improve the steadiness of his own kites. He found that if a kite-shaped hole is made at the cross-over point of the sticks, the kite is not only thereby rendered much more stable in strong winds, but also has a tendency to continue to move in any direction in which it has once been made to travel by pulls on the line, etc. Others experimented later with perforated surfaces, placing the holes in a variety of positions. In fact, a cloth-covered kite is itself a perforated kite, since a considerable amount of wind passes through the weave. The steadying effect of this easing of pressure may readily be gauged from comparing kites covered in cloth and those using sheet plastic. A plastic covered bow kite is an extremely unstable flier.

Eddy was a journalist and an amusing, extroverted showman who frequently raised flags over New York, hung lanterns in the sky at night, and generally enjoyed the publicity which was given to his harmless and often useful pastime. The other great kite-inventor of this period was a man of an entirely different stamp. Lawrence Hargrave, who was born in England in 1850 and emigrated to New South Wales when he was 16, was retiring and somewhat introverted. He freely made his scientific findings known but disliked personal publicity. In the 1880s Hargrave became interested in the problems of manned flight. During the two decades before the achievement of successful aeroplane flight he contributed many papers on the subject to various scientific and aeronautical journals. He had benefited from training in engineering and, while Eddy was essentially an enthusiastic amateur, Hargrave was a serious student of aerodynamics. He was a careful craftsman and a meticulous reporter of both his successes and his failures, records of which he kept in a voluminous series of notebooks.[2] Hargrave was a man of high, but not pompous, ethical

[1] *Monthly Weather Review*, Vol. 28, No. 12, December 1900, pp. 553–4.
[2] Now in the Museum of Applied Arts and Sciences, Ultimo, N.S.W.

principles. He believed that the taking out of patents on aeronautical discoveries was to put personal gain before the advancement of civilization. He therefore repeatedly refused to patent or make a secret of any of his work, but presented all his findings to the world as soon as possible after the event.

In his first experiments Hargrave tried to discover something about the principles of flight from the behaviour of small flying models powered by twisted rubber or compressed air. These models were primitive aeroplanes operated by either screw-propellers or flapping wings. In 1893 he began a series of experiments with kites. The general aim was to discover further information about the properties of flying

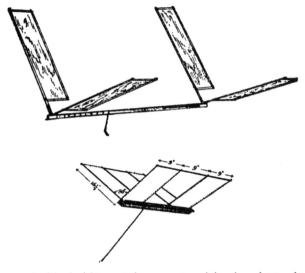

Fig. 76. Hargrave's dihedral kites, February 1893 (*above*) and March 1894 (*below*)

bodies, but he also wanted to solve the particular problem of how birds are able to soar in flight without flapping their wings. For many years Hargrave was fascinated by this question and spent a great deal of time and effort in trying to produce a kite which would advance against a breeze beyond the zenith. This, if achieved, would demonstrate the possibility of using the force of the wind to produce forward motion relative to the ground, while advancing to windward. The results of Hargrave's investigations were of doubtful value, although he did succeed in producing a series of finely shaped kites which moved as he had predicted (see below).

Hargrave's most important achievements at this time were, however, those associated with kite-design in general rather than with the soaring problem. When he first turned his attention to kites Hargrave tried a great variety of shapes. The bodies of his earlier flying models had been either flat planes or a pair of planes set at a dihedral angle. Among the first kites that he tried were some which had this same general configuration. Those shown in Fig. 76 flew fairly stably. Fig. 77 is a further dihedral kite, made of feathers, the purpose of this being to see if the stored energy in the flexing of the feathers would have any noticeable effect on the kite's action. (The results were not very conclusive.) Other experimental kites produced at about this time included those in Fig. 78.

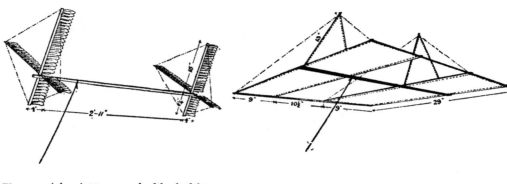

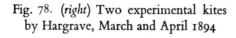

Fig. 77. (*above*) Hargrave's dihedral kite made of feathers, March 1894

Fig. 78. (*right*) Two experimental kites by Hargrave, March and April 1894

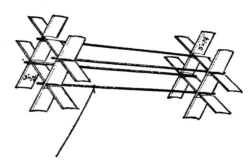

The most valuable result of Hargrave's experiments was the invention of the box kite, which he himself always called the 'cellular kite'. He applied the well-known principle, described by Wenham in his 1866 paper 'On Aërial Locomotion',[1] that two or more superposed planes may advantageously be used as lifting surfaces in place of a larger one. (A system using such superposed planes was patented by the French inventor Danjard in 1871.) Hargrave, however, hit upon the idea of placing

[1] Wenham, F. H., 'On Aërial Locomotion', in *First Annual Report of the Aëronautical Society of Great Britain*, London, 1866.

vertical stabilizing surfaces between the superposed planes. His earliest box kites contained a number of boxes, or cells, and thus resembled, as he himself said, 'two pieces of honeycomb put on the ends of a stick'.[1] Various designs of this sort, all developed in the search for stability, are illustrated in Fig. 79.

Finally it was the simple box kite with two rectangular cells which proved most useful. The construction used by Hargrave himself is illustrated in Plate 43. In various forms this kite became the standard design for meteorological work for many years, and played a large part in the development of some early aeroplanes (see Chapter 9),

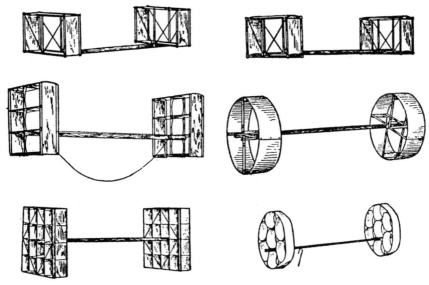

Fig. 79. Early cellular kites by Hargrave, February and March 1893

many of which were little more than powered box kites. Though not so well suited to light winds as the Eddy bow kite, Hargrave's cellular design was stronger, better able to withstand strong winds, equally efficient in a good breeze, and in most weathers proved to be the most stable kite thus far made.

Hargrave made one other contribution to kite-development at this time. It was well known that a slightly curved surface (cambered aerofoil) provided more lift than a flat one (though the reasons for this had not been adequately investigated). Hargrave accordingly built box kites with curved surfaces and, by carefully adjusting

[1] Hargrave, L., 'Flying Machines and Cellular Kites', *Journal and Proceedings of the Royal Society of New South Wales*, Vol. 27, 1893, pp. 75–81.

the curves, proved their greatly increased efficiency. The kite at the top right in Fig. 79 has curved surfaces made of tin-plate, while the kites in Fig. 80 are later designs of superior characteristics.

It is difficult to know whether Hargrave was in fact the first to make serious use of cambered aerofoil surfaces in kites. Chanute suggests that they were used as early as the eighteenth century, but there is no confirmation of this. The covers of some forms of kite (e.g., the Eddy bow) tend automatically to assume a shape approximating to the cambered aerofoil, but as far as I can discover it was not until the late nineteenth century that sustained efforts were made to develop a rigid and wholly

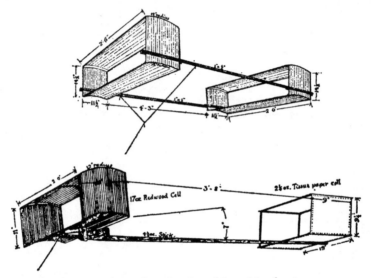

Fig. 80. Curved-surface box kites, March 1894

satisfactory kite using this principle. Most plane-surface and box kites function as 'stalled surfaces'. The high angle of attack causes turbulence behind the kite-surface, making impossible the production of lift such as that associated with the aeroplane wing. By using a cambered aerofoil, the kite can be made to fly below the stalling angle, more satisfactory lift being produced in this way. The difficulty is to achieve a design stable enough to maintain the comparatively critical angle of attack required. Hargrave himself reached something approximating to the desired results, while the beautiful wings of 'Lamson's Aerocurve Kite' (see below) represent a further step, but perhaps the most elegant cambered aerofoil kite was the Wright No. 1 glider, flown by the brothers on occasions as a ground-controlled kite.

In a paper published in 1897 Hargrave described his successes with soaring experiments, for which the apparatus illustrated in Fig. 82 was used. In order not to have his kites crash and break, he attached them to the centre of the line between the two poles, using a flying-line short enough to keep them from the ground, should they dive. He described the soaring thus:

> I stand to leeward of the poles and start the soaring kite at a positive angle, it then flies as an ordinary kite to near the zenith. The vortex then forms under the curved aluminium surfaces [Hargrave had mistaken ideas about the function of curved aerofoils] and draws the apparatus at the full stretch of the string and cord, through 180 degrees of arc to windward of the poles.
>
> The flag shows the wind to be horizontal, and the string that is plainly visible . . . shows the soaring kite pulling about 20 degrees to windward of the zenith. The wind was blowing at 12 or 14 miles per hour, which was inadequate to effect the best pull the affair was capable of.[1]

Fig. 83 is one of several non-cellular kites with which Hargrave experimented in order to achieve such soaring effects. In later years he developed a number of other

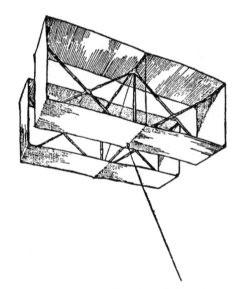

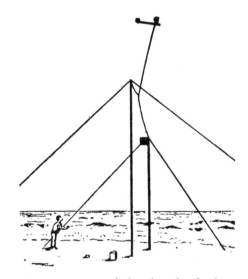

Fig. 81. The perfected cellular kite. This famous drawing is from Means' *Aeronautical Annual*

Fig. 82. Hargrave's beach poles for kite experiments, August 1897

[1] Hargrave, L., 'The Possibility of Soaring in Horizontal Wind', *Journal and Proceedings of the Royal Society of New South Wales*, Vol. 31, 1897, pp. 207–13.

kite designs, among which were a 'ladder kite' (a series of cloth cells joined directly one behind the other), and a single-celled kite with so called 'reverse curve' surfaces (shaped in a shallow 'S' from front to back, instead of the usual single concavity). Hargrave thought the latter superior to any of his other kites, but it seems never to have been developed further.

The standard Hargrave box kite, as used by meteorologists and aeronauts, was a cloth-covered wooden frame, but some of his own early models were made of heavier material, such as thin redwood sheet (e.g., the kites in Fig. 80). The success of his own kites, despite their great weight, is a tribute to their lifting power.

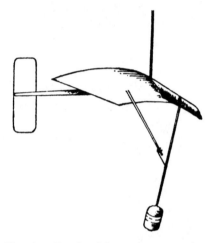

Fig. 83. Soaring kite, Hargrave, August 1898

Anyone who has flown a standard Hargrave kite about 4 feet long will know that in a moderate breeze it needs all of a strong man's powers to deal with it.

A great many variations on the basic Hargrave kite were made soon after its enthusiastic adoption by meteorologists. These variations are too numerous to mention in detail (some of them are illustrated in Fig. 84). Two basic modifications are, however, of especial interest. The first is the construction of square or diamond shaped cells, instead of the usual rectangular variety. These can be flown on their edges, which, in small kites, produces some improvement in stability. The idea was first tried by Potter, who was for some time associated with the U.S. Weather Bureau. (A similar principle was used later by Bell in his triangular box kite. See below, p. 156.) The other basic modification was the addition of 'wings', or flat

9

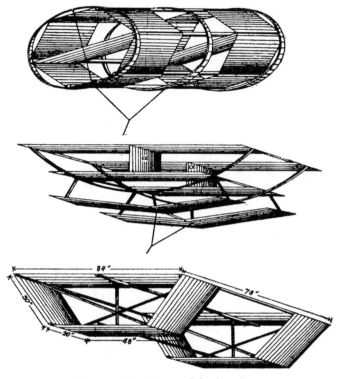

Fig. 84. Variations of the box kite

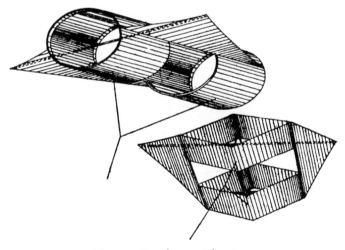

Fig. 85. Box kites with wings

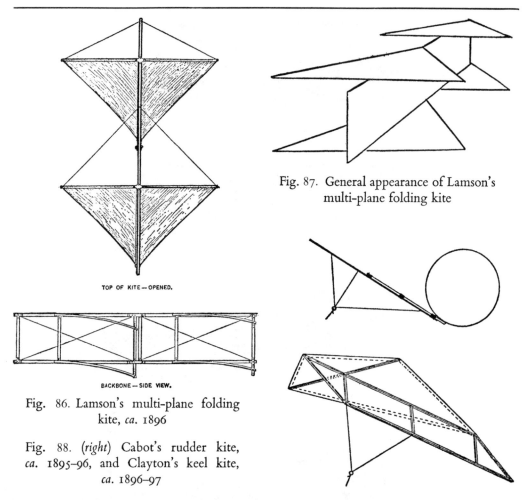

TOP OF KITE — OPENED.

BACKBONE — SIDE VIEW.

Fig. 86. Lamson's multi-plane folding
kite, *ca.* 1896

Fig. 87. General appearance of Lamson's
multi-plane folding kite

Fig. 88. (*right*) Cabot's rudder kite,
ca. 1895–96, and Clayton's keel kite,
ca. 1896–97

surfaces to increase lift (thus producing a 'compound kite'). The lower example in
Fig. 85 is one of the most effective.[1]

[1] Mr Gibbs-Smith quotes an interesting paragraph by Octave Chanute in which he claims
that he had in fact preceded Hargrave in the invention of the object for which the latter is most
renowned: the box kite. Chanute writes:

> In 1888 the present writer experimented with a two-cell gliding model, precisely similar
> to a Hargrave kite, as will be confirmed by Mr. Herring. It was frequently tested by
> launching from the top of a three-storey house and glided downward very steadily in all
> sorts of breezes; but the angle of descent was much steeper than that of birds, and the
> weight sustained per square foot was less than with single cells, in consequence of the
> lesser support afforded by the rear cell, which operated upon air already set in motion

Charles H. Lamson's major contributions to kite-flying began in 1895 when he made some of the newly publicized Hargrave kites. He experimented with various modifications and, by placing the cells slightly out of alignment, managed to produce a box kite which did not have an inconveniently strong pull.

Moving from Hargrave box kites to original designs of his own, Lamson produced a succession of kites of great elegance and efficiency. The first of these was what he called the 'multi-plane folding kite'. (The whole kite could be dismantled

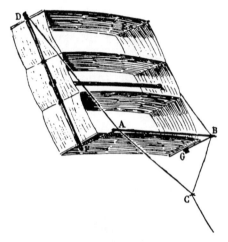

Fig. 89. Ladder-kite by Lecornu, 1898

and folded into a very small compass.) This consisted of four triangular sails, mounted on a central keel (Figs. 86, 87). Subsequently Lamson, who had undoubtedly been influenced by the biplane gliders of Octave Chanute, designed kites looking remarkably like the powered biplane of some years later. Probably the most beautiful of these, and certainly one of the most efficient, is that illustrated in Plate 43. This kite, designed in 1897 and called 'Lamson's Aerocurve Kite', was, like his earlier designs, foldable and easily portable. The front surfaces were rigidly curved by means of twelve longitudinal ribs. The flying-line was attached midway between

---

downward by the front cell; so nothing more was done with it, for it never occurred to the writer to try it as a kite, and he thus missed the distinction which attaches to Hargrave's name.

The passage is quoted from an article in the September and October, 1908, issues of *Aeronautics* (U.S.). See Gibbs-Smith, C. H., *The Aeroplane*, London, 1960, p. 318.

the point and the wings or, in a strong wind, at the forward point itself. A three-plane version of this kite was used as the leader in some of the highest flights at Blue Hill. Though not as robust as the ordinary Hargrave kite, it could operate in a gentler breeze and was therefore a very effective leader when the upper atmosphere was relatively still (Plate 57).

The only other great innovator of this period was the inventor of the telephone, Alexander Graham Bell. His work is discussed in the following chapter, in connexion with the part played by the kite in the development of the aeroplane. Certain other developments are also discussed in later chapters, but mention may be made here of a number of attempts to stabilize kites by means of rudders and keels (Fig. 88). One of the most satisfactory designs was H. H. Clayton's 'keel kite', the lower kite in Fig. 88. This was used for some time at the Blue Hill Observatory. It flies perfectly well without a tail and, if built sufficiently strongly, can withstand winds of up to 50 m.p.h.

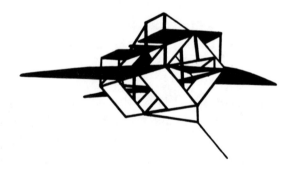

Fig. 90. Compound winged box kite, late nineteenth century.

9 | The Kite and the Aeroplane

The kite is, of course, a kind of flying machine, an aerodyne, or heavier-than-air machine. It is the oldest of all forms of aerodyne, and in the latter half of the nineteenth century, when aeronautical research was accelerating, became an important centre of interest. Even earlier it had been taken into consideration by so important an inventor as Sir George Cayley, 'the father of aeronautics', who in 1804 used a kite of the arch-top kind to build an experimental glider (Fig. 91). Gibbs-Smith describes this as 'the first modern configuration aeroplane of history with fixed main plane, and combined and adjustable rear rudder and elevator'. The following comments are from Cayley's notebook:

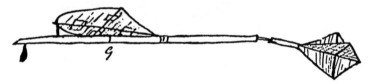

Fig. 91. Cayley's kite-glider, 1804

A common paper kite containing 154 sqr. inches was fastened to a rod of wood at the hinder end and supported from the fore part of the same rod by a peg, so as to make an angle of 6°. With it this rod proceeded on behind the kite and supported a tail, made of two planes crossing each other at right angles, containing 20 inches each. This tail could be set to any angle with the stick . . . if pointed downward in an angle of about 18°, it would proceed uniformly in a right line for ever with a velocity of 15 feet per second. It was very pretty to see it sail down a steep hill, and it gave the idea that a larger instrument would be a better and a safer conveyance down the Alps than even the surefooted mule, let him meditate his track ever so intensely. . . .[1]

Throughout his many aeronautical experiments Cayley continued to use kites and kite-forms. Fig. 92 represents a glider made from a kite. Cayley described this as

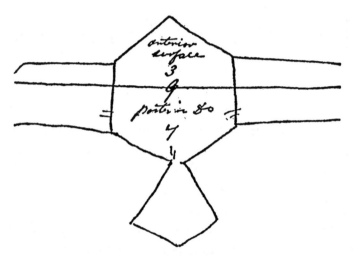

Fig. 92. Cayley's kite-glider, 1808

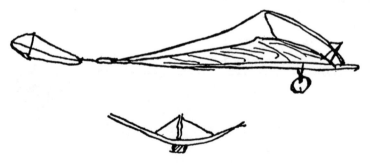

Fig. 93. Cayley's kite-glider, 1818

'a large kite formed of an hexagon with wings extended from it, all so constructed, as to present a hollow curve to the current'.[2] This model dates from 1808.

Ten years later, in 1818, Cayley made a model glider using two kites, one for

[1] Gibbs-Smith, C. H., *Sir George Cayley's Aeronautics 1796–1855*, London, 1962, p. 18.
[2] *Ibid.*, pp. 35-6,

the wing and a smaller one for the tail-unit (Fig. 93). The main kite was bowed to form a dihedral angle, in which Cayley anticipated Eddy's bow kite. Of the new design he wrote:

> A child's kite furnishes a good experiment on the balancing and steering of aerial vehicles, with a smaller one put the reverse way as a rudder stuck on by thick wire, so as to be set properly, and a weight to fasten to the middle stick till it will sail from the top of a hill slanting to the bottom, with perfect steadiness, obeying the rudder which should be turned a little up, and oblique to either side the steerage is required: the bow of the large kite should be bent up . . . by a bit of stick and a string. I have made surfaces of this kind carry down weights as high as 80 or 90 [lbs.] with perfect steadiness and steerage to either side at pleasure.[1]

Fig. 94 represents a sketch for what is probably a further kite.[2]

Fig. 94. Design by Cayley, probably for
a kite, 1839

   Cayley was defeated by the lack of a power-unit, as a consequence of which his direct use of kites was primarily in connexion with gliders. When power finally became available in small enough compass, the aeroplane arrived–and it was essentially a combination of two basic aeronautical devices: the screw-propeller (for traction), and the kite-surface (for lift). (Interest in the potentialities of the rigid lifting surface had of course to compete against the old obsession with flapping wings.)

   Kites were taken into consideration by virtually all those who experimented with heavier-than-air machines in the latter part of the nineteenth century. Typical of the early designs using rigid kite surfaces, to which power was added, is Fig. 95, due to Thomas Moy. Moy was an imaginative and not altogether unsuccessful

[1] *Ibid.*, p. 85.
[2] *Ibid.*, p. 101.

precursor of the inventors of the aeroplane proper.[1] The figure represents a small flying model which he produced in 1879 and exhibited at a meeting of the Aeronautical Society. He described it as a 'military kite' mounted on wheels and provided with propelling gear. (In 1892 Moy patented an ingenious military kite which doubled as a parachute.)

The flying of kites was one stage in the carefully graded experiments of the Wright brothers. In August 1899 they built a biplane kite which they flew from a

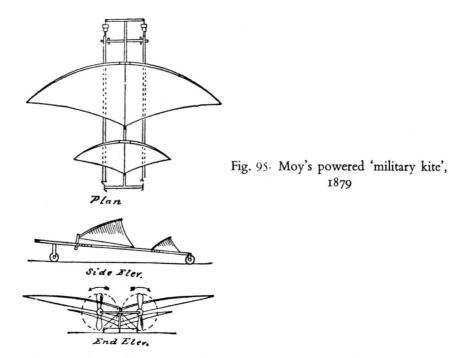

Plan

Side Elev.

End Elev.

Fig. 95. Moy's powered 'military kite', 1879

system of lines used to experiment with the control of lifting surfaces. This important kite is illustrated in Fig. 96. The control lines enabled the wings to be warped either up or down, that being the beginning of the wing-warping lateral control which was to characterize Wright aeroplanes for years to come. This was followed by work with their 'No. 1 glider' (1900) which was flown principally as a kite. The kite and the glider were basically biplane structures but, unlike Hargrave's box kites (see pp. 138-9), they had no vertical stabilizing surfaces between the wings, stability being maintained by the control lines.

[1] See Gibbs-Smith, C. H., *The Aeroplane*, London, 1960, p. 21.

The Wrights' work with kites soon gave way to trials with gliders proper. From the point of view of the kite-enthusiast, however, the work of two other aeronautical experimenters of the same period continued for longer to be of special interest. The first of these men is of course Hargrave, while the second is Alexander Graham Bell, whose grandiose investigations were of little value to the development of the aeroplane, but produced some of the most startling kites ever seen.

In his striving after the aeroplane, Hargrave, like so many others, put stability before manœuvrability. The first aim was to produce a machine capable of lifting a

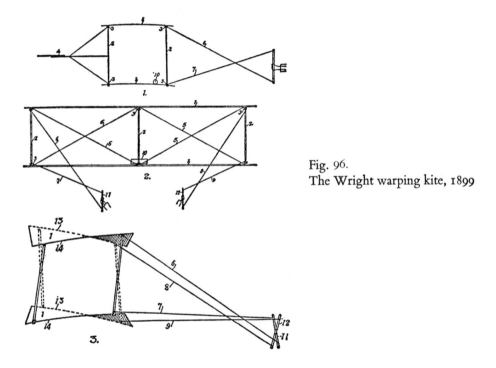

Fig. 96.
The Wright warping kite, 1899

man into the air and sustaining him there in safety despite the vagaries of the wind or accidental shifts in centre of gravity, etc. As soon as this had been achieved, power might be added, provided that a light motor could be obtained. As Mr Gibbs-Smith has pointed out, the real break-through in aeroplane design came when the Wright brothers consciously chose unstable supporting surfaces which had to be controlled by the aviator to keep them flying. Hargrave, however, working at the problem of inherent stability, helped to make possible the development of aircraft which, in good conditions, were stable, but were difficult and slow to manœuvre. His own ascent in 1894 was associated with very little danger and, as he frequently pointed out, the retaining line of the train of man-lifters could, both in theory and in practice, have been replaced by a motor. The plan was that the kites should be raised with the line anchored to the ground. The motor, attached either at or below the lowest kite, would then be started, facing to windward, the anchor would be hauled up and the journey begun. Since the motor would necessarily be light in weight, the whole thing could be portable:

> The particular steps gained are the demonstration that an extremely simple apparatus can be made, carried about, and flown by one man; and that a safe means of making an ascent with a flying machine, of trying the same without any risk of accident, and descending, is now at the service of any experimenter who wishes to use it.[1]

Hargrave even suggested that the system could be set up from the top of a bus.

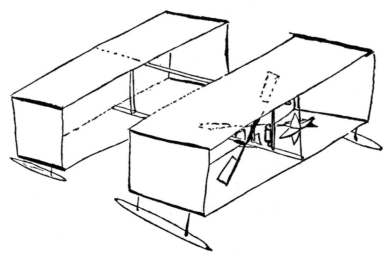

Fig. 97. Design for a box-kite aeroplane, Hargrave, 1896

The powered man-lifters never, apparently, received a trial in practice, but the Hargrave kite itself was made the basis of more than one practical aeroplane. Gabriel Voisin (who later set up an aeroplane factory with his brother Charles) helped to design two float gliders in 1905, in co-operation with Archdeacon and Louis Blériot. These gliders were subsequently developed further to become some

[1] Hargrave, L., 'Paper on Aeronautical Work', *Journal and Proceedings of the Royal Society of New South Wales*, Vol. 29, 1895, p. 47.

of the first successful European aeroplanes. The gliders were basically Hargrave kites, with several large cells in front, and one or two smaller cells at the rear. The well-known Voisin aeroplanes, developed from these beginnings, were, in the first powered versions, free of the Hargrave 'side-curtains' on the main wings, but acquired them later, in 1908. As late as 1910 these side-curtains were still being used, to produce stability. The Europeans were slow to abandon the idea of inherent lateral stability, but the increasing use of ailerons or wing-warping for control in roll caused the box kite curtains finally to disappear altogether. Their disappearance, coinciding with the adoption of true manœuvrability in European aeroplanes, also

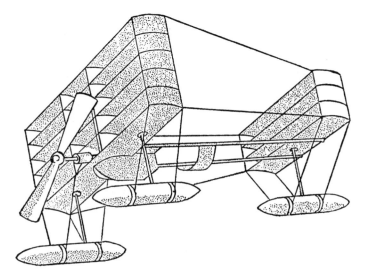

Fig. 98. Design for a box-kite aeroplane, Sidney Hollands, 1902.
Based on ideas from Hargrave.

removed a cause of instability and unpredictability in cross-winds. It must be stressed that ailerons and side-curtains were not, of course, mutually exclusive. Santos-Dumont (see below) added ailerons to one version of his '14-bis', while in 1908 Farman fitted them to his side-curtained Voisin machine, but the adoption of full lateral control soon rendered the curtains redundant and a nuisance.

The Santos-Dumont aeroplane just mentioned received a good deal of publicity in 1906. It was the first to fly publicly in Europe, though it made, in fact, only a hop of 722 ft. in its best flight. The grotesque and ugly machine, designed by Santos-Dumont himself, flew 'backwards', i.e., with the smaller cell leading. It consisted basically of a system of Hargrave box kites set at a dihedral angle. A pusher propeller was used.

At this point, in order to remove a possibility of confusion, mention must be made of the aeroplane known as the 'Bristol Box-kite' (1910). This well-known name was an unfortunate choice, since the aeroplane concerned had nothing whatever to do with the earlier box-kite configuration of Voisin, etc.

S. F. Cody (see Chapter 10) produced an early rudimentary aeroplane by adding power to a modification of one of his fine large box kites. This kite with

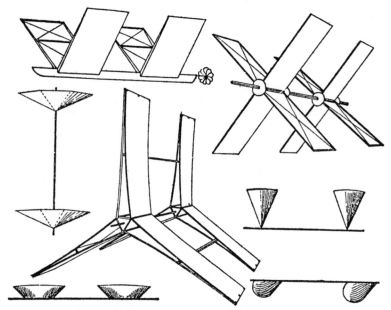

Fig. 99. Bell's spool kites and radial kites, early 1898

engine (called by Walker and Gibbs-Smith the 'motor-kite') is not to be confused with the 'Cody power-kite'. The latter term was used by Cody to describe a Wright-derived aeroplane of his design, having nothing directly to do with kites. The 'motor-kite' achieved in 1907 the small distinction of making a pilotless powered flight along a wire.[1] Later, of course, Cody became one of the most successful of the early pilots flying in the British Isles.

Alexander Graham Bell, best known as the inventor of the telephone, was born in Scotland in 1847 but spent many years in Canada and later became a citizen of the

[1] Thought, until recently, to have been a free flight.

United States. He was early interested in the problems of manned flight and, like Joule, cultivated his scientific interests even on his honeymoon (1877), when he made notes on the flight-patterns of crows. From 1898 to 1910, when aeronautical work was progressing rapidly in various parts of the world, Bell experimented with kites of various shapes. Some of the earliest of these are illustrated in Fig. 99. The criteria of the flying-machine he had in mind were set out as follows:

> In order that there may be safe ascent and descent, it seems to me necessary that the machine must have the power of hovering in the air at any desired height, and of ascending and descending slowly without horizontal velocity.
>
> In order that there may be translation from place to place, the machine must also be capable of horizontal motion in any desired direction.

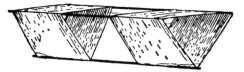

Fig. 100. Bell's triangular box kite, *ca.* 1898

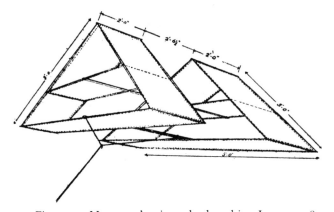

Fig. 101. Hargrave's triangular box kite, Jan. 25, 1894

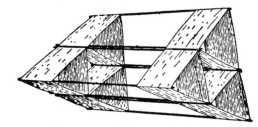

Fig. 102. Bell's compound triangular box kite, *ca.* 1900

In order to try to realize his aim, Bell set about developing a kite that would be strong, light, and above all stable. Such a kite would be provided with a propeller or propellers as motive powers. (In 1909 and 1910 he experimented with propeller-driven kites.) Bell's researches resulted in his making and testing an immense number of kites of very varied design. A great article in *The National Geographic Magazine*[1] illustrates these with some ninety photographs and diagrams.

Bell began from the Hargrave box kite, which he called 'the high-water mark of progress in the nineteenth century'. For his purposes, however, Bell found that he needed a kite that was structurally more rigid but which could nevertheless be made

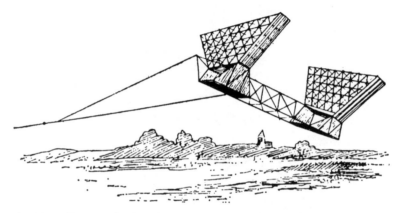

Fig. 103. Multi-cell triangular box kite. (Drawing from a contemporary photograph)

large enough to carry a man without becoming prohibitively heavy. The first step was the development of the 'triangular box kite' (Fig. 100). This is structurally stronger than the rectangular version and is of comparable efficiency. It flies with one flat side uppermost, so that one of the sticks functions as a stabilizing keel.

It is interesting to note that Hargrave tried kites of very similar shape. One, with cambered aerofoils made of tinplate, was unsuccessfully tried on March 9, 1893, while another (Fig.101) was flown inverted on January 25, 1894.

One of the great virtues of Bell's arrangement was that a number of such kites could be combined to form a larger compound kite, as in Fig 102. Furthermore, since there is clearly no need to retain both of the longitudinal sticks where two of

[1] Bell, A. G., 'The Tetrahedral Principle in Kite Structure', *The National Geographic Magazine*, Vol. 14, No. 6, June 1903, pp. 219–51.

these lie alongside one another, as shown in the figure, the ratio of surface to weight for the larger kite may actually be better than for the single-celled version. This is of course not the case when a normal Hargrave kite is simply increased in size, since area and weight increase respectively as the square and the cube of the length.

Bell in fact experimented with huge compound kites of this type, but found them unsatisfactory for a number of practical reasons. The most serious objection to a large compound kite of this kind is that as the number of cells increases so the

Fig. 104. A single tetrahedral cell

distance between the cells must increase, which results in a very large dead load due to the weight of the sticks in the middle. Bell tried various other ways of combining single triangular cells, producing, among other designs, a series of curious kites with the cells arranged radially, like sectors of a wheel.

The major advance, however, and the kite design for which Bell became best known, was the reduction of the triangular cell to the shape shown in Fig. 104. This is the shape of the regular tetrahedron. As each side is triangular, it is inherently rigid, and needs no bracing. (Bell used this shape to build many things besides kites.) Any two sides of such a tetrahedron may be covered, and the single cell can be made

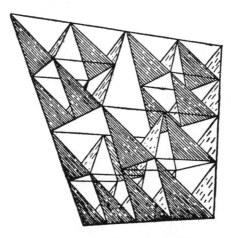

Fig.105. A 16-cell tetrahedral kite

to fly from a bridle attached to each end of the stick around which the cover bends.

It is clear that any number of such cells can be connected together without changing the surface-to-weight ratio (e.g., Fig.105). At first Bell thought that he would have to leave spaces between clusters of cells, but later discovered that such was not the case.

By 1905 he had made a kite capable of lifting a man. This he called the 'Frost King'. It consisted of 1,300 cells, each about 10 ins. on a side. The whole thing weighed only 61 lb., was about 18 feet long and 9 feet wide. It was equipped with a rope ladder to which on one occasion a man clung. Including the man and the

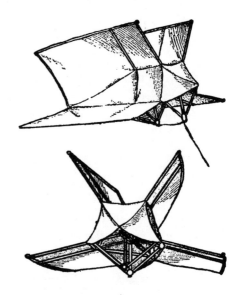

Fig. 106. (*above*) Sketch by Bell for a
powered tetrahedral kite

Fig. 107. Zimmerman's kite, 1898

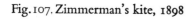

equipment the total weight lifted was 227 lb., and the height reached was about 30 feet.

The 'Frost King' was, however, only a beginning. In 1907 Bell built a tetrahedral structure that made the 1905 version look diminutive and one which must rank among the largest kites ever to fly. The 'Cygnet', as he called it, consisted of 3,393 cells. (Beinn Bhreagh, near Bell's laboratory, gained a new industry as workmen and seamstresses turned out the thousands of silk covers.) The kite was to be launched by a steamer on Baddeck Bay, Nova Scotia, for which purpose it was equipped with light floats. In the centre was an opening for a man. Bell hoped to test the kite with a passenger aboard, after which he planned to install an engine to replace the steamer's power. On December 6, 1907, the kite was launched with Lieutenant

10

Thomas E. Selfridge of the U.S. Army aboard. (Later he was to be killed, in the first fatality in the history of powered flight.) For seven minutes it flew beautifully, and was then allowed to settle on the water. The Cygnet had risen to 168 feet and descended so slowly and gently that Selfridge, whose vision was obscured by the structure, did not realize that he was dropping until the kite reached the surface. Unfortunately for Bell, the line to the tug was not released quickly enough. The Cygnet was dragged through the bay and destroyed, but Selfridge escaped with a wetting.

The work of Bell, and the development of the box kite, were only two of the many direct applications of the kite to the needs of powered flight. Even quite late in the history of flying there were dozens of lesser men who attempted to develop the kite in the hope of achieving a practical aeroplane. Among these was Charles Zimmerman, who designed the curious kite illustrated in Fig. 107. Zimmerman wrote the following description:

> The wings are rigid in front and flexible in the rear. A bicycle wheel is beneath to run on the ground. The frame is of steel tubing and bamboo covered with sheeting, and spreads from 190 to 210 square feet of sustaining surface, or about one square foot to every pound of weight to be lifted and carried. When open it is from 12 to 15 feet long and 8 to 10 feet wide and high. When closed it presents a bundle similar to an umbrella 8 to 10 feet long. Its weight is from 25 to 35 lbs.
>
> Through many experiments it is found that this machine safely and evenly rides or sails through the air without deviating to the right or left unless so directed by the operator, who by bearing his weight on one side can steer to that side. It will go up or down, always with the right side up, no matter how the wind blows. It sails at a flat angle with the horizon, and often advances against the wind as though pushed by some unseen force.[1]

The kite was to be powered by a method which Zimmerman was not 'at liberty, at present, to make public'. That, as far as I can discover, was the last that was ever heard of the idea.

[1] Zimmerman[n], C., 'A New Form of Aeroplane', *The Aeronautical Journal*, Vol. 2, No. 3, July 1898, pp. 64-5.

10 | Military Kites and Other Uses

Although they were two thousand years behind the Asian generals, western experimenters were no less enthusiastic and ingenious in suggesting that the kite might be a useful addition to military equipment. During the nineteenth century in particular there was a flood of patents for systems, many of which were highly imaginative and impractical. Most involved either traction or man-lifting.

Among early military applications was one devised by Admiral Sir Arthur Cochrane during the Russian War, in 1855. He made some trials with twelve-foot kites to see if they might be used to tow torpedoes to a target. The trials were very successful, the kites travelling fast and accurately over distances of about two miles.[1]

Cochrane's suggestion was of practical value, but a system devised by A. M. Clark, and patented in 1875, demonstrates just how fanciful inventors could be. Fig. 108 is Clark's illustration of an imaginary observation kite which he devised. Needless to say, the kite is entirely impracticable.

As I mentioned in Chapter 7, Baden-Powell made a serious contribution to the development of man-lifting kites for military use, but it was not until S. F. Cody developed his system that military kites became a wholly practicable possibility in England. Cody, born in the United States in 1861, was a flamboyant and amusing showman who eventually settled in England and adopted British nationality but never lost anything of his colourful personality. (He was a friend, but not a relative, of 'Buffalo Bill' Cody.) From his youth Cody was interested in the possibility of flight and hoped for many years to be the first man to achieve it. Although he did not fulfil that ambition, he succeeded in producing a very satisfactory system of man-lifting box kites and later became a highly skilled pilot.

[1] *The Aeronautical Journal*, Vol. 2, No. 1, Jan. 1898, p. 4.

65. Bell's 'Cygnet,' 1907.

66. Bell's 'Cygnet II,' 1909.

67. Bell's ring kite, 1908.

68. Bell with some of his kites at the St Louis Exhibit, 1904.

69. Saconney military kite (French, *ca.* 1910).

70. Winch for the Saconney kite.

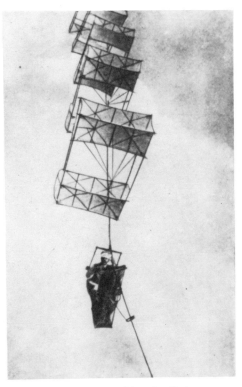

71. Saconney kites in flight.

72. Schreiber man-lifting kites, 1903.

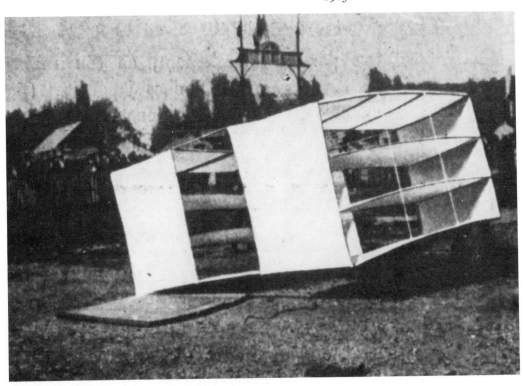

73. Multi-cell box kite, *ca.* 1900.

74. Kites used for signalling. Pocock, early nineteenth century.

76. David Thayer's life-saving kites used to tow a raft, *ca.* 1890.

75. Life-saving kites. Pocock, early nineteenth century.

77. Box kite used in 'Gibson Girl' survival equipment, World War II.

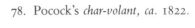
78. Pocock's *char-volant, ca.* 1822.

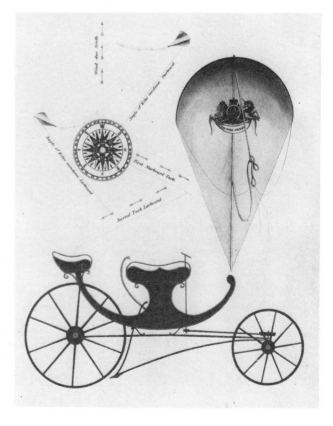

79. Patent illustration for the
char-volant.

80. Paul E. Garber with one of his steerable target kites, World War II. *Smithsonian Institution*

81. Ski-kite, Perth, Western Australia. *West Australian Newspapers, Ltd*

82. Aero-kite. *The Harmon's*

84. Rogallo kite with rigid members, used as a ski–kite. *Sydney Morning Herald*

83. Rogallo flex–wing kite. *NASA*

85. Ski-kite with floats. *Sydney Morning Herald*

86. Rogallo flex–wing test-bed vehicle.

87. Jalbert parafoil being used for meteorological observations. NB the flight angle, showing the parafoil's remarkable efficiency.

88. Decorative Conyne kite.
Julia Hedgecoe

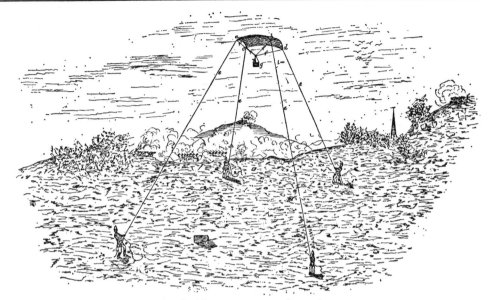

Fig. 108. Clark's imaginary military kite, 1875

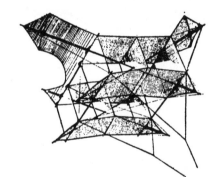

Fig. 109. Cody's 'Bat' kite, *ca.* 1903

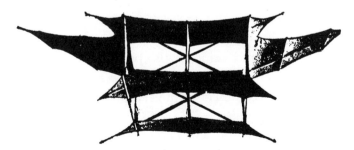

Fig. 110. Another version of the Cody kite, *ca.* 1904

Cody carried out a succession of experiments with kites of various configurations, but finally settled on the design illustrated in Figs. 109 and 110. These 'bats', as they were called, were twin-celled Hargraves, with wings for added lift. The Cody system, which set the pattern for many man-lifting designs in other parts of the world, involved, first, the flying of a train of kites to provide initial lift, after which a further kite, beneath which a man was suspended, seated in a wicker chair, was allowed to travel up the line on a trolley. The ascender was able to control the ascent and descent by means of a system of lines and brakes. He was also equipped with a camera, a telescope, a firearm, and a telephone for maintaining contact with the ground. With equipment of this sort Cody sent a Lieutenant Groslie to what seems

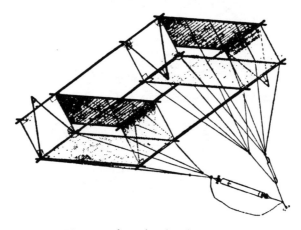

Fig. 111. The Schreiber kite, 1903

to be a record height for a kite ascension: 1,200 metres. (In 1909 Groslie suffered a terrible fall from a man-lifter.)

This system, which was patented as early as 1901, interested the British War Office. Extensive trials with the equipment were carried out from 1903 to 1905, some of them from warships which had been put at Cody's disposal by the Admiralty. Finally, in 1906, the War Office adopted the perfected system for the Army. It remained part of British military equipment for some years but became redundant, of course, with the rapid development of the aeroplane.

Man-lifting systems of a similar type were developed at about the same time by other countries, including Russia and France. Early in the century the Russians adopted a system of man-lifters for their navy. This, designed by Lieutenant

Schreiber, consisted of six or seven Hargrave kites functioning in a wind of from 10 to 20 metres per second. The Schreiber kites were soon abandoned because of a series of fatalities caused by unstable flights. Another Russian officer, however, Captain Ulyanin, developed a ground-based system which was used by the Russian army. Ulyanin used a more satisfactory train of double Conyne kites (triangular box kites with wings).

Interest stimulated by the English experiments resulted in the holding of a competition in France, in 1909, run by Dollfus. The competition, which was intended to discover the most satisfactory system for possible use in the French armed services, was won by Captain Madiot, who produced a system using winged rectangular box kites. Development of this was stopped by the unfortunate death of Madiot in

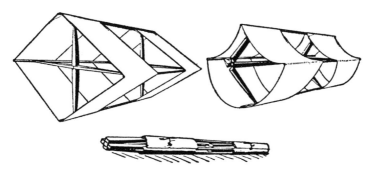

Fig.112. Early German man-carrier, used in the First World War

an aeroplane accident the following year. The French army subsequently made use, however, of a man-lifter designed by Captain Saconney. His kites were very similar to Cody's and employed Cody's method of ascension. The observer was hauled aloft along the main lifting line by a set of kites towing a nacelle. Saconney's kite-corps was equipped with motor-car, trailer, and winch–the last being driven by the car's engine. (The kites were also tried aboard ship–the *Edgar Quinet*–in 1911.)

The Germans continued to use the man-lifting war kite longer than any other nation. During the First World War they vastly increased the observational range of their U-boats by flying a man-carrier above the surfaced vessel. The kite, an elegant folding box design (Fig.112), was, of course, independent of natural winds, since a sufficient breeze could be created by the submarine itself. After launching, the basket with its occupant was hauled up, using a man-powered winch. The look-out officer was able to regulate his position on the cable by manipulating a set of brakes and pulleys.

The problems involved in getting a man down quickly in case of accident or emergency led the Germans to develop other military kites of rather safer design. In one of these the observer sat within the kite itself, on a keel-like structure. By suitably disposing his weight the observer could convert the kite into a glider. Another of the many observation-kites used by the Germans was of the parachute type. This was little more than an obliquely arranged parachute which, if the line were severed, descended as a true parachute in the normal way.

During the Second World War the Germans once again made use of kites for observation from U-boats. This time the apparatus used was of a much more highly developed kind. The kite consisted of a set of rotating blades supporting an observation chair and amounted, in fact, to a type of surface-powered autogiro.

Man-lifting and the traction of torpedoes are not, however, the only military uses to which kites have been put. Some other applications, such as the distribution of pamphlets and letters, are mentioned later in this chapter. Since at least as early as 1911, kites have been used as gunnery targets,[1] but perhaps the most valuable of all military uses was their application by allied forces during the Second World War for the barrage-protection of convoys. The U.S. Navy adopted them in 1941, using box kites which had originally been designed for advertising displays. These were perfected for their new role by H. C. Sauls, of the War Shipping Administration. The kites were flown on lines 2,000 feet long, from which the barrage wires were suspended.

OTHER USES OF KITES

(1) *Traction.* The use of kites to pull boats, carriages, sleds, and other objects is one of their earliest practical applications. According to Morwood,[2] kites were used by the Samoans to pull their canoes from one island to another, while one of the first instances recorded in the west is a boyhood experience of Benjamin Franklin:

> I amused myself one day with flying a paper kite; and approaching the bank of a pond, which was near a mile broad, I tied the string to a stake, and the kite ascended to a very considerable height above the pond while I was swimming. In a little

[1] *Aeronautics* (London), Vol. 4, No. 10, Oct. 1911, p. 201.
[2] Morwood, J., *Sailing Aerodynamics*, Southampton, 1962, p. 87.

time, being desirous of amusing myself with my kite and enjoying at the same time the pleasure of swimming, I returned; and, loosing from the stake the string with the little stick which was fastened to it, went again into the water, where I found that, lying on my back and holding the stick in my hands, I was drawn along the surface of the water in a very agreeable manner. Having then engaged another boy to carry my clothes round the pond, to a place which I pointed out to him on the other side, I began to cross the pond with my kite, which carried me quite over without the least fatigue and with the greatest pleasure imaginable. I was only obliged occasionally to halt a little in my course, and resist its progress, when it appeared that by following too quick I lowered the kite too much; by doing which occasionally I made it rise again. I have never since that time practised this singular mode of swimming, though I think it not impossible to cross in this manner from Dover to Calais. The packet-boat, however, is still preferable.[1]

In the early nineteenth century kites were used to provide traction in case of shipwreck. This subject is treated separately, below.

Probably the most spectacular early use of the kite for traction was that of George Pocock, whose man-lifting operations have been discussed in Chapter 7. He designed a special light-weight carriage, drawn by kites, which was given its first road test on January 8, 1822. The idea was patented by Pocock, in collaboration with James Viney, in 1826 (Plate 79). The kites used were of a special design, improving on the common English arch-top. They were foldable, having joints in the wings and in the spine, and were provided with movable distenders by means of which the wings were spread. Furthermore, the kites, which were flown in train, were manipulated by four lines which effectively controlled their lateral and longitudinal angle to the wind and made it possible to fly them to either side of the current. In this way the carriage could be pulled across the wind.

Although the kites were designed in the first place to pull the carriage (*charvolant*, as Pocock called it, modifying French *cerf-volant*), it was later suggested that they might be used to pull many other things besides, including ships, and for the raising of flags, signals, weights, etc. Pocock relates that he experimented, as a child, with drawing stones along the road by means of a kite, and that in later years he made a sled out of a board 72 ins. by 15 ins. on which one of his sons was seated. A kite was attached to the board, which was dragged away with remarkable speed. Pocock describes the subsequent chase:

---

[1] Franklin, B., *Benjamin Franklin's Autobiographical Writings*, sel. and ed. C. van Doren, New York, 1945, pp. 3–4.

Mazeppa's wild horse was as easy of control. The young solitary *Laplander* courageously kept his seat, the Kites dragging him and his novel vehicle over hillocks, and ruts, and beds of furze, till he arrived at the opposite extremity of the Downs, where, descending into a stone quarry on his well-poised sledge, he alighted at the bottom (as it happened) in perfect safety, and when his panting pursuers, who had 'toiled after him in vain', arrived at the goal, they found the fortunate adventurer still seated on his car, exulting that he had kept possession of his runaway equipage, and that he had so distanced his comrades in the race. By this first perilous journey it was learnt, that no horse or rein-deer in car or sledge could successfully compete with Kites in speed, and also that no mode of travelling would be so dangerous and precarious, unless the Kites could be controlled and the vehicle directed and stopped.[1]

Pocock's first trial of the practical system that grew out of those early experiences took place on a large pond belonging to the Earl of Suffolk. A small pleasure boat was pulled across the water, with quite some success.

Soon afterwards there came the tests of the *char-volant* itself. Pocock claimed speeds of up to 20 m.p.h., and on one occasion indiscreetly passed the carriages of the Duke of Gloucester. (The breach of etiquette having been noticed, the *char-volant* was made to slow down so that the Duke, courteously recognizing the gesture, might pass.) On another occasion Pocock's party overtook the stage-coach between Bristol and Marlborough.

A typical pair of kites, used to draw a carriage containing four or five persons, were respectively twelve and fifteen feet high, the smaller acting as pilot, or leader, kite.

The effects of this horseless carriage on the populace were often quite dramatic. Pocock comments:

> It has happened too, that after such flights new and strange tales have been told of the fiend having been abroad; that the prince of the power of the air had certainly been let loose, and was now driving nightly up and down on the earth.[2]

An added bonus was exemption from toll-fees. Pocock relates an incident:

> . . . on one occasion an old inquisitive lady-like turnkey refused to open the gate to a party with the *Char-volant*. Hearing a carriage rattle up to the bar, she ran hastily out; but on seeing no animals attached to the vehicle, she started and stared,

---

[1] Pocock, G., *The Aeropleustic Art*, London, 1827, p. 11.
[2] *Ibid.*, p. 31.

and after a short pause, exclaimed, 'Why, gentlemen! what d'ye go by? what is it that draws you?' The Kites were pointed out to her aloft in the air, and then, for the first time, she noticed the string fastened to the car. 'What,' she added, 'do they draw you along? Do they indeed!! Well, what must I charge you, gentlemen? What d'ye call them?'–'Kites, Kites!'–'They ben't horses!' 'Oh, no.'–'Nor mules!' 'No.' 'And I'm sure they ben't donkeys, nor oxen!' Then looking up at her toll-board, she observed, 'Kites! Kites! why there be nothing about Kites on my board–so I suppose you must go along about your business!'[1]

Together with his children Pocock made use of his kites in other parts of England, causing quite a stir. At Ascot, in 1828, he attracted the attention of George IV, while in July of the same year, at the Liverpool Regatta, a two-masted boat was sailed by kites across the Mersey to Birkenhead and back, at one stage beating into the wind. (Some people find it difficult to understand how a kite, sailing to leeward, can pull a boat to windward. The principle is in fact no different from that involved in beating to windward with a fixed sail, as Morwood[2] points out. In recent times Morwood himself made some experiments with kites for sailing to windward and developed a new form of rig based on the idea.) The use of kites for pulling boats was both suggested and tried many times after Pocock. One of the most celebrated trials of the idea was made by Cody who, in 1903, sailed successfully across the Channel with his modified box kites, so confirming Franklin's supposition.

Pocock was in fact not the only one to make use of a *char-volant*. A Mr William Yates drove one through Manchester on July 30, 1828. The vehicle could make only about 2 m.p.h. uphill, but rolled at a brisk pace along the level.[3]

(2) *Life-Saving Kites*. From as early as 1760 inventors had proposed the use of life-saving kites in case of shipwreck. They were based on the idea (already seen in the case of the Cordner kite discussed in Chapter 7), that shipwreck usually occurs on a lee shore. Perhaps the earliest really practical device of this kind was one designed in 1821–22 by Captain C. C. Dansey of the Royal Artillery.[4] This kite was to be flown to land, carrying a grapnel. When well over the shore it was to be caused to fall, so that the grapnel might make itself fast. The kite proposed was of the English

[1] *Ibid.*, pp. 37–8.
[2] Morwood, *op. cit.*, pp. 86–8.
[3] 'Traction by Kites', *The Engineer*, Vol. 90, Aug. 24, 1900, p. 193.
[4] Dansey, C. C., 'Kite for effecting a communication between a stranded ship and the shore', *Transactions of the Society For the Encouragement of Arts*, Vol. 41, 1825, pp. 182–9.

diamond variety, but with an interesting modification. The cover was made square, and the lower sections of cloth lying outside the outline of the kite were to be left free, to operate as steadying wing-flaps (Fig. 113). (Later experiments by James Means showed, however, that flaps of this sort have no beneficial effect.)[1] The cloth for Dansey's kite was 9 feet on a side, and a tail five or six times the length of the kite was attached. The spine was furnished with a two-leg bridle, the lower leg of which was held by a catch that was released when struck by a messenger sent up at the appropriate time. The kite thus fell to the ground and the attached grapnel was

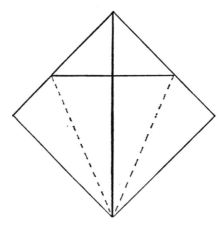

Fig. 113. Structure of Dansey's kite with wing-flaps, 1821–22

made fast. This apparatus was tried and found satisfactory, which resulted in Dansey's being awarded the gold medal of the Society of Arts. It is not known, however, whether the kite was ever used in case of actual shipwreck.[2]

One of the most successful of life-saving designs was produced by Captain (later Sir George) Nares. *The Daily Graphic* ran a competition for life-saving devices which Nares won with the kite illustrated in Fig. 114. This was to be flown to shore, like the Dansey kite, and it too was to be brought down when it had reached land. The method of landing was, however, superior to Dansey's. A second line was to be passed through a ring at the junction of the bridle and the flying line. If the wind were

[1] Means, J., 'The Kite Considered as an Instrument of Value', *The Aeronautical Annual*, 3 vols., Boston, 1895–97, Vol. 2, pp. 112–3.

[2] Much later in the century Dansey's idea was plagiarized, with some modifications, by a J. D. Hickman: see 'Life Saving Devices', *Scientific American Supplement*, Vol. 34, 1892, p. 13803.

Fig. 114. Nares' life-saving storm-kite, 1861

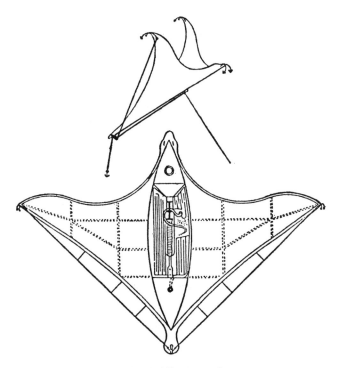

Fig. 115. Chatfield's storm-kite, 1892

blowing directly on to the shore, this second line was to be attached to the bottom of the kite. Pulling the line, when the kite was over the land, upset the balance and brought it down. If the wind were oblique, however, the line was to be attached to one of the side-corners of the kite. Manipulation of the line, during the kite's flight, guided it into the wind, and so to land. Pulling harder upset the kite and brought it to the ground as before.[1]

As may be seen, this kite was an anticipation of the Bell tetrahedral. It was spread by the stick at the back, the amount of spread being suited to the strength of

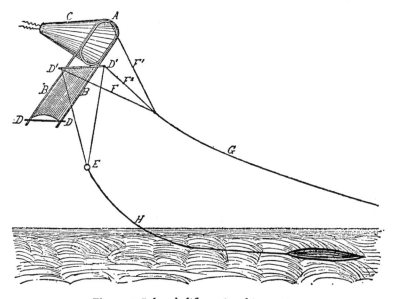

Fig. 116. Jobert's life-saving kite, 1887

the wind. A tail was used, consisting of a series of wind-cups (see below, p. 182), which Nares invented.

Fig. 115 is a further storm-kite, designed by a Mr Joseph Chatfield.[2] It was intended to drag a buoy to shore.

An excellent life-saving device, of quite sophisticated design, was produced in 1887 by Jobert, a well known French kite experimenter (Fig. 116). It is not dirigible, as the Nares kite is, but it has several advantages. The angle of the lower,

[1] Nares, Sir G., *Seamanship*, Portsmouth, 1886, pp. 276–80.
[2] 'Life Saving Devices', *Scientific American Supplement*, Vol. 34, 1892, p. 13965.

flat part can be varied according to whether it is desired to fly the kite high or to let it carry the line out almost horizontally. The trailing line (H) with the buoy attached serves not only to steady the kite but also to provide something for rescuers on land to grasp. At the back of the cone are two pieces of metal foil which vibrate in the wind and make a loud humming noise to summon help.[1]

Figure 117 represents a much simpler life-saving kite designed by the American, Woodbridge Davis. As shown, it is dirigible through a wide arc, the control being

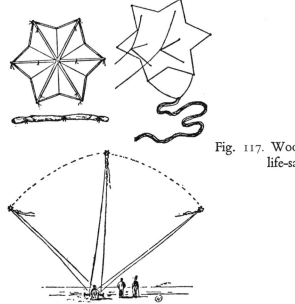

Fig. 117. Woodbridge Davis' dirigible life-saving kite, 1894

exercised by varying the tension on the two lines from which it is flown. The kite folds up into a compact bundle.[2]

(3) *Photography*. For a short time photography from kites became immensely popular among kite-enthusiasts. The first photograph to be taken from a kite seems to have been the work of E. D. Archibald, whose meteorological studies are dis-

[1] Jobert, C., 'Un cerf-volant porte-amarre à cone', *l'Aéronaute*, Vol. 20, No. 3, March 1887, pp. 43–6.

[2] Davis, J. W., 'Some Experiments with Kites', *Aeronautics* (New York), Vol. 1, No. 11, Aug. 1894, pp. 153–6.

cussed above. In 1887 he took a number of photographs, using a small explosion to release the shutter. Many other methods of shutter release were developed later by such people as William Eddy, and the two Frenchmen, Emile Wenz and Arthur Batut. Most of the literature on kite-photography is now of only historical interest. Photography from aeroplanes has made the technique outmoded and in any case the development of smaller and lighter cameras has made the often cunning suspension devices no longer relevant. A detailed account of the methods current by the end of the nineteenth century is to be found in Lecornu's book.[1]

(4) *Miscellaneous.* There have been countless minor applications of kites. They have been used to carry telephone wires and to raise wireless antennae.[2] They have been used for carrying rocket flares, for signalling, even for releasing homing pigeons.

The use of kites as a means of communication between two groups of people has had some interesting developments. In Paris, in 1870, a kite was used by smugglers, who by this means bypassed the gates of the city wall and introduced contraband liquor. A rather more ethical form of communication by kite is the leaflet-raid carried out in thirteenth-century China and discussed on p. 25, above. It is almost impossible that Lord Dundonald should have heard of this leaflet raid, but he seems to have hit upon the idea independently when, during the Peninsular War, he communicated with the French from his ship, using a kite carrying proclamations. (The latter were released by a slow-burning match.)[3] A further example of the same technique was seen during the American Civil War:

> A novel mode of giving light to benighted rebels on the subject of the President's 'Amnesty' has recently been tried with success along our lines. A common boy's kite is sent skyward and rebelward whenever the wind is favorable, having two strings, one strong and the other weak. To a particular weak spot in the weak string a bundle of printed promises of amnesty is fastened. When the kite is high enough and soaring far within rebel lines, the stout string is slackened and all the strain is brought upon the weak. Instantly the cord parts at the tender spot, and the proclamations, 'thick as autumnal leaves which strew the streams in Valombrosa',

[1] Lecornu, J., *Les Cerfs-volants*, Paris, 1902.

[2] Marconi's famous trans-Atlantic transmission, on December 12, 1901, from Poldhu in Cornwall to Signal Hill, Newfoundland, was made possible when the aerial was raised some 400 feet by means of a kite. The aerial wire itself was 600 feet long.

[3] Dundonald, T., *The Autobiography of a Seaman*, 2 vols., London, 1860, Vol. 1, p. 201.

shower gently o'er hill and plain and forest top, where the rebels can pick them up. Is not that a brilliant thing, and worthy of universal Yankee ingenuity?

[This is said to be an invention of General Butler's.][1]

(As the Chinese example shows, General Butler was more than a little late with his invention.)

The Confederates showed that they also could make good use of a kite, but this time to provide a primitive form of airmail. The description of this event is taken from the Washington *Republican*:[2]

> A large kite is made, covered with oiled silk to render it impervious to sea water. Folded letters and newspapers are tied in loops along the tail. When the tail is as heavy as can conveniently be carried aloft, a cord long enough to reach two-thirds of the way across the river is attached, and the kite flown. After the kite has exhausted the string, the cord is cut and the kite allowed to be borne by the wind the remainder of the distance, and descends on the Virginia shore, where people are waiting for the load. With the first favorable wind, back comes the kite to Maryland.

In all these experiments, the kite-line was fixed and stationary at the bottom end. Experiments in communication using travelling kites were conducted some time later. In 1906 S. H. R. Salmon of the Aeronautical Society made some trials to see whether cross-Channel communication were practicable. From Brighton he released three box kites, pulling drags, and bearing messages asking the finders to communicate with him. One of these was never heard of again; one fouled a fishing vessel at Berck, 75 miles away; the third travelled as far as Vierville, having covered more than 103 miles in $11\frac{1}{2}$ hours.[3]

A somewhat less humane use of the kite is that which involves game animals. The Chinese are said to have used kites with loud hummers to drive game. During the nineteenth century in England and France they were often used to hunt game birds, particularly grouse and partridge. Lord Onslow wrote:

> When I was a boy kites were used (and may be still) in shooting partridge late in the season when the birds are still very wild and too scarce for driving. The birds when they saw the kite overhead ran into the hedgerows. Two guns walked on

[1] *Scientific American*, Vol. 11, No. 6, Aug. 6, 1864, p. 82.

[2] 'Airmail in the Civil War', *Civil War Times*, May 1964, p. 37.

[3] Salmon, S. H. R., 'Across-Channel Communication by Kite', *The Aeronautical Journal*, Vol. 10, No. 3, July 1906, pp. 44–5.

each side of the hedge and the birds were flushed by a spaniel. It is poor sport only useful for getting a few birds for the pot.[1]

Another sportsman, writing in the same year, suggested that the partridge eventually learned that kites were not dangerous and that the method therefore grew ineffi-cacious, but it seems more likely that a process of natural selection took place. The

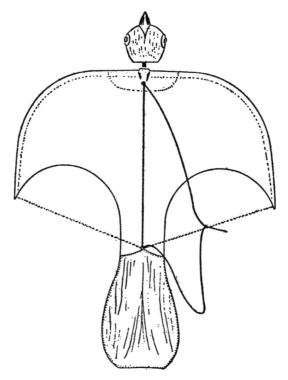

Fig. 118. Collapsible hunting kite, 1884

kites used for the sport varied in their verisimilitude. Fig. 118, a collapsible hunting kite patented in 1884 by I. K. Rogers, was among the more lifelike.

An imaginative suggestion for extending the use of the hunting kite was included in a note which appeared in *The Gentleman's Magazine*:

The diversion of kite-flying, which, tho' omitted by *Ainsworth*, probably as a childish thing, . . . cannot be justly consider'd as the mere pastime of boys; since

[1] *Notes and Queries*, Vol. 182, No. 11, March 14, 1942, p. 152; see also Vol. 182, No. 16, April 18, 1942, p. 223.

the ingenious Mr *Condell*, who has imitated the figure and motion of the living kite in the paper one, frequently amuses himself with flying it, as well as severall other persons, who are men, as far as age and stature can make them so.–To render this contrivance useful as well as entertaining, he hints (among other fancies) that a good artificial kite, dextrously play'd, may keep partridges couched on the ground till the net can be drawn over them; and that the likeness of the Duke of *Cumberland* flown over the Highlands would have the same effect on the skulking rebels.[1]

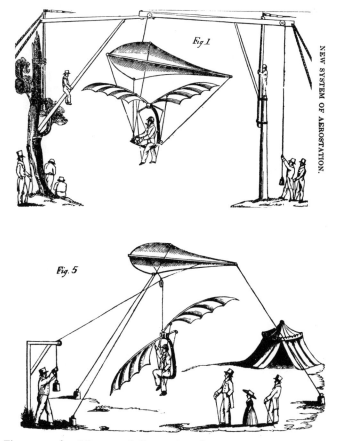

Fig. 119a, b. Kites used for testing flying apparatus, 1829.

[1] *The Gentleman's Magazine*, Vol. 16, 1746, p. 431; quoted from the *Westminster Journal*, Aug. 16, 1746.

11 | Flying Techniques

In addition to the development of the kite itself, it is useful to consider the history of the techniques and apparatus used for its launching, flying, and landing.

THE BRIDLE

As the function and purpose of the bridle are not always well understood, it may be helpful to summarize these first.

In general, the bridle regulates the angle between the kite and the wind. If we assume that the kite remains at a constant height, and that the angle of the line to the ground is therefore constant, the following degrees of control may be exercised:

(i) There may be no bridle at all, but the point of attachment may be so chosen that the resultant of wind and gravitational forces maintains a satisfactory fore-and-

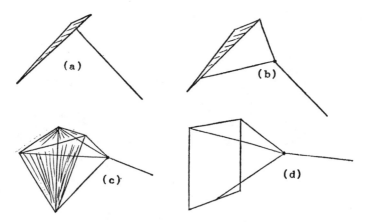

Fig. 120. Bridling techniques
176

aft angle between the kite and the ground (Fig. 120a). The kite is free to move in any direction around the point of attachment. The lateral angle will be dependent mainly on the relative pressures of the wind on each side, and the longitudinal angle on gravity and wind-pressure.

(ii) A two-leg bridle, fixed to the spine, allows the kite the same lateral freedom as in (i), but the longitudinal angle is now under some control from the strings. If the kite should change its angle, a much greater turning moment comes into play to return it to its original position. (The geometry of this does not concern us. Interested readers may consult the exhaustive treatment in C. F. Marvin, *The Mechanics and Equilibrium of Kites*, Washington, 1897.) Thus, for a given position of the towing point, the kite is held virtually rigid in the fore-and-aft direction, while still having considerable freedom to rock from side to side (Fig. 120b).

(iii) Addition of lateral bridle strings, as in Fig. 120c, provides lateral stability similar to the longitudinal stability just mentioned. If the kite is of suitable shape, the four legs may be reduced to three, with the same effect (Fig. 120d).

(iv) For the virtually complete control of (iii), partial control in either or both directions may be substituted. This may be accomplished by introducing a compliant or elastic component into the bridle string. A rubber-band or spring in the lower leg of a two-leg bridle, for instance (Fig. 121), will stretch when the wind-pressure on the kite increases. This will cause the kite to diminish its angle of attack until the wind subsides. A similar effect occurs if no bridle is used, but in the present case the controlling effect of the bridle is still largely retained – only gusts cause a change of angle, and this may be of great benefit.

(v) Varying degrees of control by means of bridle-lines may be combined with compliance in the structure of the kite itself. The kite's effective angle may be varied by changes of shape caused by changing wind-pressure.

The orientals, as we have seen, used quite highly developed bridling methods. I know of no evidence that they ever hit upon the elastic bridle, but they applied all the other methods of control so far mentioned. The multi-point attachment of the kite in Fig. 12 is equivalent to the four-leg bridle; the Nagasaki kite uses a two-leg bridle, and also bends in the wind to regulate the pressure; the rectangular Japanese kites in Figs. 8 and 9 are held rigid in the centre, but are allowed to flex at the edges, so adding to the stability.

In the Pacific, bridling seems never to have reached any state of perfection. Some of the fishing-kites in Fig. 23 use simple bridles, while a few, like the kite from the Carolines (Fig. 24), use a four-leg bridle. As far as I can determine, however, the large Maori bird-kites were flown without any form of bridle, which is one reason for their notorious swooping (and dangerous) flight.

In the west the bridle was developed only slowly towards a satisfactory state. The earliest known European kite, that described in Vienna codex 3064, has no bridle at all, properly speaking, but the system of rings along the face of the dragon allows for varying points of attachment, depending on the force of the wind. While this is already a considerable advance on the single-point attachment still often used centuries later, it provides for no regulation of the kite's angle during flight, except for that due to the balance of gravitational and wind forces around a single point.

The set of rings on the Vienna kite is nevertheless an impressive device when compared with the crude methods of attachment specified for many German and Italian kites of the sixteenth and seventeenth centuries. In the majority of cases the flying line is tied only to the crossing of the sticks. The bridling of della Porta's kite is, however, an outstanding exception, using what is still today the standard method of attaching a three-leg bridle to a rectangular or hexagonal kite.

The illustration in Bate (Fig. 49) shows a two-leg bridle, but the draftsman had evidently no very sound idea of its function. The upper string is drawn loosely and uselessly drooping. If the draftsman ever flew a kite himself he must have used the old single-point attachment of the line.

A two-leg bridle was always used on the imported Javanese pear-kite, but only in the eighteenth century do we find the two-leg bridle becoming the standard method of attachment for other kites. The use of the 'belly-band' attached at or near the top and bottom of the spine has continued to be the norm in children's two-stick flat kites to this day. Eddy used a two-leg bridle for his bow kites, attaching the strings to the cross-over point and to a point near the bottom of the spine. The use of these points of attachment has the advantage that the wind-pressure on the surface of the kite tends to bend the spine less than with the alternative two-leg bridle attached at the extremities of the spine. Eddy made his kites flexible in the lateral direction in order to achieve a certain measure of self-regulation under wind-pressure. It was found, however, that this flexibility had too great an effect on the kite's efficiency, and more rigid structures were soon substituted. The bow kite can be flown satisfactorily direct from the cross-over point, without any bridle, and it may be steadied in the lateral direction by the use of a four-leg bridle (first used by J. B. Millet).[1]

Hargrave normally worked entirely without a bridle, attaching his line to an optimum point found by trial. When his kites were adopted for meteorological work, however, it was found advisable to use bridles in order to achieve added stability in conditions of varying wind. Two-, three-, and four-leg bridles were commonly used, and in some cases a multiplicity of legs was tried in order to help maintain rigidity in the kite's structure (see Fig. 111).

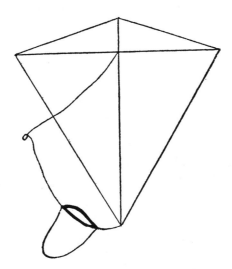

Fig. 121. Simple elastic bridle

One of the most significant advances in bridling techniques was the invention of the 'elastic bridle' mentioned above. This was devised independently by several people around 1890.[2] By its use a kite can be set to pull by only a fixed amount in the strongest wind. Sudden increases of tension on the flying line and associated apparatus are thus avoided. Using this device, the Blue Hill people were sometimes able to fly their kites in winds of 50 or 60 m.p.h.

[1] Millet, J. B., 'Scientific Kite Flying', *The Century Illustrated Monthly Magazine*, Vol. 54, No. 1, May 1897, p. 68.

[2] Clayton, H. H., 'A Keel Kite', in *The Aeronautical Annual*, 3 vols., Boston, 1895–7, Vol. 3, p. 151; Chanute, O., *Progress in Flying Machines*, New York, 1894, p. 196.

MULTIPLE LINES

The amount of control that can be exercised over a kite by using a single bridle is, of course, limited. It is impossible to say who first conceived the idea of increasing the control by flying more than one line but this has certainly been done for a long while in China. As pointed out above (p. 130), bird-kites sometimes have independently controllable wings.

In the west, the use of two lines may have been first conceived by Dansey for his life-saving kite (see pp. 167-8). Pocock's kites were, however, the first to make practical use of multiple-line control. His four lines, attached to the four extremities of his kites, afforded him complete control over their attitude in both the fore-and-aft and lateral directions.

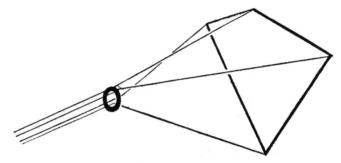

Fig. 122. Multiple lines. (The line to the top of the kite is fixed to the ring. The other three pass freely through it)

After Pocock the use of multiple lines was frequently suggested. Birt found three lines of great assistance in steadying his hexagonal kite (see p.107), and Nares, like Pocock, used multiple lines to achieve genuine manœuvrability. Each of these experimenters seems to have arrived at his end-point independently, due no doubt to the lack of any widely distributed information about what had been done with kites in previous years. Fig. 118 illustrates how two lines were manipulated to vary the position of the Woodbridge Davis kite.

The most remarkably successful multiple-line system was not, however, developed until during the Second World War, when Paul Edward Garber of the Smithsonian Institution, then in the Navy's Bureau of Aeronautics, designed a kite for use as a gunnery target. It used two lines, wound on synchronized reels. At the bottom of the spine of the kite (a modified Eddy bow) was a rudder which was controlled by tension on the lines. By manipulation of the rudder the kite could be made to perform virtually all the evolutions of an aeroplane (except for the roll), as seen from the ground. The kite was produced by the thousand during the war and has since been adopted by many kite enthusiasts.[1] (See Plate 80.)

Garber's gunnery target is the most sophisticated controllable kite yet devised. Other attempts at using rudders, both before and since, have been markedly less successful. Further mention must, however, be made of the 'warping kite' devised and flown by the Wright brothers. (See above, p. 123.) By varying the position of the four lines attached near the kite's extremities, the Wrights were able not only to

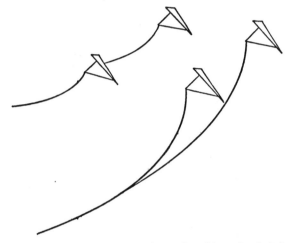

Fig. 123. Two methods of flying in train: *above*, the old method; *below*, Eddy's method

warp the surfaces to simulate the twisting of the wings of a soaring bird, but were able also to adjust their relative position in the fore-and-aft direction. This manipulation adjusted the overall centre of pressure and had the further effect of varying the angle of incidence of a horizontal elevator ('rudder', as they called it) attached to the rear centre upright of the kite.

FLYING IN TRAIN

Schoolboys during the nineteenth century flew trains of kites as a normal part of the sport, but it cannot be said with certainty how long before that the technique had

[1] Grahame, A., 'Target Kite Imitates Plane's Flight', *Popular Science Monthly*, Vol. 146, No. 5, May 1945, pp. 65-7.

been used. Alexander Wilson used a train in the important experiment of 1749, but this did not, of course, become generally known until the publication of the memoir, in 1826.

Colladon devised the system independently in 1827, flying three kites joined at their backs. Pocock connected his kites in the same way, and so, later, did Hargrave when experimenting with his man-lifters. (Hargrave's system of connexion is the same as that in the illustration of 'Jimmy's' flight, Fig. 69.) Eddy, however, seems to have been the first to fly in train by using separate lines for each kite, these being connected one by one to the main line. This method he adopted in 1890 or 1891.[1] The two techniques of flying in train are illustrated in Fig. 123.

Fig. 124.
Nares' wind-cup

TAILS

The tail was one of the few parts of the kite which did not reach any high degree of sophistication in the east – due, of course, to the general use of tailless kites. With the adoption of the box kite in the west the tail became redundant there as well, but in the second half of the nineteenth century tails of great efficiency were developed for traditional kites.

Sir George Nares, whose life-saving kite is discussed in the preceding chapter, made a substantial improvement to the heavy-weather performance of flat and bow kites by the addition of a tail composed of self-adjusting wind cones (Fig. 124). These are small cones of paper or heavy cloth which may come to a point at the bottom, or be truncated as in the illustration. The stronger the wind, the greater the

[1] Eddy, W. A., 'Experiments with Hexagon and Tailless Kites', *Aeronautics* (New York), Vol. I, No. 11, Aug. 1894, p. 152.

resistance provided by such a tail. The wind-cone tail was later adopted by Archibald and others to steady the movement of meteorological kites.[1]

Another tail worthy of special mention is that used by Teisserenc de Bort in the early days of the Trappes observatory, when flat hexagonal kites were being flown. This tail, very valuable for use with any flat kite to which it can be attached, is made as shown in Fig. 125. The cross-pieces are lengths of light wood, or other rigid material, while the vertical parts of the 'ladder' consist of twine or tape. This tail damps the sideways rocking movements of a kite. (Cf. the della Porta kite, p. 83.)

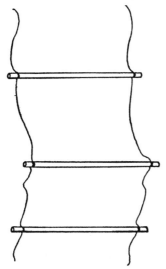

Fig. 125. Tail used by Teisserenc de Bort,
1890s

LANDING TECHNIQUES

Experienced fliers know that when landing a kite in a strong wind one may more satisfactorily bring it down for the last hundred feet or so by anchoring the line and walking out toward the kite, pushing the line down as one goes. This technique, known as 'underrunning' the kite, was developed by meteorological fliers who sometimes used a small wheel, attached to a handle, which they placed on the wire to make the landing easier. It is of great interest to notice that the underrunning technique is described in Vienna codex 3064. The author suggests that the line be held down under one arm while walking out to the kite, and that the other hand be kept

[1] Fergusson, S. P., 'Exploration of the Air by Means of Kites', *Annals of the Astronomical Observatory of Harvard College*, Vol. 42, Pt. 1, 1896, p. 54.

on the line in case it should break (because of the extra strain caused by this landing method).

GROUND-POWER

The boy who runs with his kite in order to create an increased wind-pressure is producing the simplest form of ground-power-assisted flight. Methods of achieving such assistance for practical reasons have been varied, including the use of ships (used by meteorologists), horses, and at least one motor-car. Le Bris's galloping horse may have given a hint to Bell, who once flew one of his giant kites in that way,[1] while Baden-Powell, of course, as mentioned on pp. 123-25, had some unfortunate experiences with horse-drawn kites. The only motor-car power that I know of was used in 1898 by Emile Wenz. Having in mind some improvements in the techniques of kite-photography Wenz tried to develop a method of flying a five-foot hexagonal kite from a car, but nothing further seems to have been done with the idea after the initial successful trials.[2]

Undoubtedly the most important use of ground-power was for meteorological observations at sea. As has already been pointed out (p 112) Dines and Shaw used a ship off Crinan to make many of their observations early in this century. Rotch, of the Blue Hill Observatory, also made a series of widely publicized observations from ships. These had the advantage that a launching wind was always available, and that by altering the course of the ship a great deal of control could be exercised over the kite's flight.

Nowadays, of course, the most common form of powered kite is the water-skier's man-lifting sail.

Perhaps the oddest suggestion for developing flying techniques was made by Carl Myers in 1892.[3] Having succeeded in making and flying tailless kites, he next

[1] Bell, A. G., 'The Tetrahedral Principle in Kite Structure', *The National Geographic Magazine*, Vol. 14, No. 6, June 1903, p. 230.

[2] Wenz, E., 'Note sur l'enlèvement d'un cerf-volant par un temps calme au moyen d'une automobile', *l'Aéronaute*, Vol. 32, No. 4, April 1899, pp. 87-90.

[3] Myers, C. E., 'The Texas Dynamite Kites and Application of Kites to Aerial Photography', *Scientific American Supplement*, Vol. 33, No. 835, Jan. 2, 1892, pp. 13348-9.

proposed to make a kite fly without a string. Myers had failed to understand the system of forces which maintains a kite in the air and suggested that it should be possible to balance a kite so that the string would become redundant. If his system could have been made to work, perpetual motion would at last have been achieved!

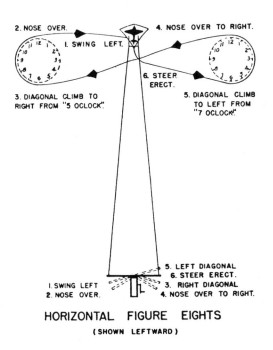

Fig. 126. Control diagram for Paul Garber's target kite, World War II.

12 | Modern Kites

After a period of neglect during the early decades of the twentieth century, kites have once again caught the imagination of aeronautical engineers and technologists generally.

One of the most interesting developments is the perfecting of the 'flexi-kite', which is entirely without a rigid frame. The first such kite of which I have any knowledge was flown by Baden-Powell some time before 1894, when he was experimenting to find the best form for a man-lifter. Unfortunately he gave no details of the design, beyond saying that he succeeded in getting it to fly. The modern non-rigid kite is due to Francis Rogallo, of the National Aeronautics and Space Administration, Virginia. In 1945, after the end of the Second World War, Rogallo began research on flexible wings. His early work was carried out privately, since at that time no organization was willing to subsidize such experimentation. Rogallo, who has always been a keen kite-flier, was trying to develop a kite with the stability of shape of a parachute, but with the lift of an aeroplane wing. Before the end of 1948 he had succeeded in producing the first fully successful flexible-wing kite, which he called the 'Flexi-Kite'. A patent application was filed in 1948, and allowed in 1951.

Rogallo did not, however, cease development of his kite at that point. At first he continued privately, having freed himself from dependence on the weather by installing a 36-in. electric fan in his house. This was arranged so as to produce a strong draught through a doorway, thereby providing him with a simple wind-tunnel. The earliest flex-wing kites used a tail consisting of a windsock (actually the bag in which the kite was stored when not being flown). Later Rogallo developed kites that could be flown with or without tails in light winds, though they still require tails if the wind is strong.

The flexi-kite is held in shape by means of a system of shroud lines, forming a multi-leg bridle (Plate 83). Rogallo's first kites needed as many as twenty-eight shroud lines, but owing to their tendency to tangle, he designed simpler models using first six and later as few as four lines. These kites are extremely light and efficient. They respond to wind-pressure to take on an almost perfect aerodynamic shape, being somewhat like a highly cambered supersonic wing. Since they use no sticks, they are virtually unbreakable.[1]

Although the flexi-kite was first used as a toy, and continues to be very popular, the principle involved was later put to more serious use. Rogallo's flex-wings were accepted by two American aircraft companies, Ryan and North American, for potential application as gliders and dirigible parachutes, and as the basis of a new sort of manned vehicle. In 1961 the testing was completed of the first powered manned flex-wing test bed. This led soon afterwards to the development of a 'Fleep', a flying jeep, which can work from short, rough landing surfaces, and will lift loads of close to half a ton.[2]

The large flex-wings used in these applications have the same general configuration as the Rogallo kites, but they are provided with rigid frame members. (In some applications these members are simply inflated cylinders of flexible material.) A flex-wing of this sort can, like the original frameless Rogallo design, be flown without a tail as a very efficient, fast-moving, and beautiful kite.

During the last few decades the most common use of the kite has of course been for sporting and recreational purposes. The fishing-kite, imported into England more than half a century ago, has more recently been popularized in the U.S. by such well known fliers as Will Yolen (President of the International Kitefliers Association). A still more recent use, which seems to have begun in Jamaica, is as an aid to water-skiing. The skier, holding a bar beneath a large, tailless kite, is raised into the air by the wind produced by the speed-boat. The kite (Plate 81) is a modification of the standard lozenge. On September 19, 1965, two Frenchmen, Jacques Gofreville and Bernard Danis, crossed the English Channel on ski-kites. The crossing took 65 minutes, the kites flying non-stop at about 100 feet over the water.

New kites are continually being devised. The number of possible shapes is limitless, and the methods of flying and controlling them have by no means been exhausted. Some years ago L. W. Bryant carried out detailed research on the design

[1] Rogallo, F. M., 'First Flexible Kite', *Ford Times*, March 1951, pp. 25–9.
[2] ' "Fleep" Flight Tests Complete', *Ryan Reporter*, Vol. 25, No. 2, Summer 1964, pp. 18–19.

of a stable and efficient rigid kite. Like Rogallo, Bryant used a wind-tunnel and evolved an elegant biplane kite with swept-back wings.[1]

Recent developments in sporting and recreational kites have included the introduction of the Jalbert Parafoil (and the related Sutton Flow Form and Ferrari Ram kites), a series of "Marconi-rigged" kites (first popularized by W.M. Angas), the Allison-Scott "sled," the Jones and Merry Flexifoil, the Professor Waldof box kite and the Robinson Facet kite (both designs indebted to Hargrave), a stream of "stunter" kites controlled by dual lines (initiated by Peter Powell), and the "roller" and others from David Pelham's book *Kites*—along with reels, books, clubs and journals that seem to be proliferating.

Kite Lines, the quarterly journal of the worldwide kite community, documents and promulgates new ideas. Communication among enthusiasts is increasing and competition for world records in kiting has become an international game. (For example, the "Largest Kite," achieved in Japan in March 1980 with an area of 2,950 square feet, was overtaken in the United States in October 1980 with a Parafoil of 3,500 square feet, only to be superseded in the Netherlands in August 1981 with a new inflatable design of 5,952 square feet. There is no denying the innovative energy of such enthusiasts.) The growing body of international kiters is doing much to eradicate the popular idea that kites are merely children's toys. Long may it thrive.

Fig. 127. Experimental kite used by Lilienthal and his brother, 1874

[1] Bryant, L. W., *et al.*, *Collected Researches on the Stability of Kites and Towed Gliders*, London, 1950.

A Summary Chronology

1847	Birt's trials at Kew.
ca. 1850	Disappearance of the Maori kite.
1859	Cordner lifts a man?
1868	Le Bris and his coachman are lifted.
1876	Simmons' trials.
1883	Archibald experiments with meteorological kites.
1885–6	Maillot tries his man-lifter.
1887	First kite photographs (Archibald).
1891–2	Eddy devises his bow kite.
1893	Hargrave's box kite.
1894	Baden-Powell lifts a man; first automatic recording instruments raised (Eddy at Blue Hill); Hargrave lifts himself.
1896	Wise makes the first U.S. ascent.
1899	Hargrave brings his box kites to London, and lectures on them.
1901	First western kite-fishing?
1905	First application of the box kite to a full-size aeroplane (Voisin-Archdeacon float-glider).
1909	First death due to kite-flying?
1910	Train of ten kites reaches 23,385 ft. (Mount Weather, Va.).
1919	Train of eight kites reaches record height of 31,955 ft. (Lindenberg).
1933	Meteorological kites no longer used in the U.S.
1945–8	Rogallo invents the flex-wing kite.

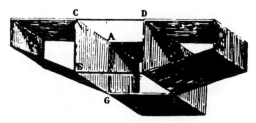

Fig. 128. Russian compound box kite, late nineteenth century.

Bibliography

I have tried to list all books on kites published in English, together with the principal books in other European languages. No such attempt has, however, been made with articles. The literature on kites has, since about 1890, been very extensive indeed. As most of the articles deal, in much the same ways, either with meteorological kites or children's kites, I have listed only a representative selection of some of the best. Furthermore I have not attempted to list separately the many notes and brief articles from journals in which constant reference is made to kites. In these cases I have included only articles of special importance, or articles actually referred to in the course of this book. A list of some of the more important journals will be found at the end of the bibliography.

Many books about the east and the Pacific contain brief mentions of kites, ranging from one word to a page or two. There are literally hundreds of such books, whose inclusion would unduly encumber the bibliography. A selection only of these is given here. Readers wishing to pursue this subject further should consult the references in Plischke and Chadwick (see below).

Unsigned articles are listed by title.

A brief indication of the nature of the contents of entries has been included where it seemed useful to do so.

Children's books are indicated by 'Ch' in parentheses after the entry.

Works of special importance are indicated by an asterisk (*) before the entry.

ABBREVIATIONS USED

AJ (*The Aeronautical Journal*)
JAI (*Journal of the [Royal] Anthropological Institute of Great Britain and Ireland*)
JPRSNSW (*Journal and Proceedings of the Royal Society of New South Wales*)
MWR (*Monthly Weather Review*)
NGM (*The National Geographic Magazine*)
SA (*Scientific American*)
SAS (*Scientific American Supplement*)

Abbe, C., 'Espy and the Franklin Kite Club', *MWR*, Vol. 24, No. 9, Sept. 1896, p. 334.

— 'The Franklin Kite Club', *MWR*, Vol. 24, No. 11, Nov. 1896, p. 416.

— 'Sir Isaac Newton and his Kites', *MWR*, Vol. 24, No. 12, Dec. 1896, pp. 458–9.

★— 'The Development of the Kite by European Scientists', *MWR*, Vol. 25, No. 2, Feb. 1897, pp. 58–61.

— 'The Franklin Kite Club', *MWR*, Vol. 25, No. 4, April 1897, pp. 162–3.

— 'The Kite as Used by Espy', *MWR*, Vol. 25, No. 4, April 1897, p. 163.

— 'Spool Kites and Kites with Radial Wings', *MWR*, Vol. 27, No. 4, April 1899, pp. 154–5.

— 'Evolution of the Meteorological Kite', *MWR*, Vol. 42, No. 1, Jan. 1914, pp. 39–40. (The above is only a selection of a lengthy series of articles published in *MWR* by Cleveland Abbe, for some time the journal's editor.)

'Aérostats et aéronefs, ou nouveaux principes de la navigation aérienne', *Le Magasin Pittoresque*, Vol. 12, No. 21, 1844, p. 166.

'Airmail in the Civil War', *Civil War Times*, May 1964, p. 37.

Almela y Vives, F., *Folklore de . . . altura; cometas en el cielo de Valencia*, Valencia, 1947.

The Americana, New York, 1911, Vol. 11, 'Kite', 'Kites in War'.

Ammianus Marcellinus, *Rerum gestarum libri qui supersunt*, XVI, 10, 7 (Loeb, Vol. 1, pp. 244, 245).

Andersen, J. C., *Maori Life in Ao-tea*, Christchurch, 1907, pp. 270, 421 (Kite-songs).

★Anell, B., *Contribution to the History of Fishing in the Southern Seas (Studia Ethnographica Upsaliensia*, IX), Uppsala, 1955 ('The Fishing Kite', pp. 29–41).

Angas, W. M., 'Unique Tailless Kite', *Popular Science Monthly*, Vol. 137, No. 1, July 1940, pp. 176–7.

— 'Marconi-Rigged Kite Soars in a Breeze', *Popular Science Monthly*, Vol. 151, No. 5, Nov. 1947, pp. 170–3.

Archibald, E. D., 'An Account of Some preliminary Experiments with Biram's Anemometers Attached to Kite Strings or Wires', *Nature*, Vol. 31, No. 786, Nov. 20, 1884, pp. 66–8. (See also Vol. 31, No. 809, April 30, 1885, p. 600; Vol. 33, No. 860, April 22, 1886, pp. 593–5.)

— *Les cerfs-volants militaires*, Paris, 1888.

'An Ascent with Tandem Kites', *SA*, Vol. 76, No. 5, Jan. 30, 1897, p. 68. (Wise's first ascent.)

★Babington, J., *Pyrotechnia*, London, 1635, pp. 44–6.

Baden-Powell, B. F. S., 'Present State of Aeronautics', *AJ*, Vol. 1, No. 1, Jan. 1897, pp. 4–5.

★— 'Man-Lifting War Kites', *AJ*, Vol. 1, No. 2, April 1897, pp. 5–8.

★— 'Kites: Their Theory and Practice', *AJ*, Vol. 2, No. 2, April 1898, pp. 33–45.

★— 'War Kites', *AJ*, Vol. 3, No. 1, Jan. 1899, pp. 1–6.

— 'The War Kite', *McClure's Magazine*, April 1899.

— 'Man-Lifting War Kites', *Aeronautics* (London), Vol. 4, No. 5, May 1911, pp. 53–4; No. 6, June 1911, p. 89; No. 9, Sept. 1911, p. 167. (Later thoughts on man-lifters.)

Balfour, H., 'The *Goura*, a Stringed-Wind Musical Instrument of the Bushmen and Hottentots', *JAI*, 1st s., Vol. 32, 1902, pp. 170–2. (Humming kites in the east.)

★— 'Kite-Fishing', In *Essays and Studies Presented to William Ridgeway*, Cambridge, 1913, pp. 583–608.

' "Barrage Kites" Shield Convoys', *Popular Science Monthly*, Vol. 145, No. 2, Aug. 1944, p. 125.

★Bate, J., *The Mysteryes of Nature and Art*, London, 1634, pp. 80–2.

Batut, A., *La Photographie aérienne par cerf-volant*, Paris, 1890.

Bayne-Powell, R., *The English Child in the Eighteenth Century*, London, 1939, p. 218.

Bell, A. G., 'The Tetrahedral Principle in Kite Structure', *NGM*, Vol. 14, No. 6, June 1903, pp. 219–51.

★— 'Aërial Locomotion', *NGM*, Vol. 18, No. 1, Jan. 1907, pp. 1–34.

'The Bell Tetrahedral Kite in Wireless Telegraphy', *SA*, Vol. 94, No. 16, April 21, 1906, p. 324.

Bertinet, E., *La Théorie élémentaire du cerf-volant*, Paris, 1887. (Of no importance.)

Best, E., 'The Diversions of the Whare Tapere', *Transactions and Proceedings of the New Zealand Institute, 1901*, Vol. 34, pp. 34–69.

★— *Games and Pastimes of the Maori*, Dominion Museum Bulletin No. 8, Wellington, 1925, pp. 67–81.

Bodde, D., *Annual Customs and Festivals in Peking*, Peiping, 1936, pp. 77, 78.

Boesch, H., *Kinderleben*, Leipzig, 1900, Figs. 75, 85.

★Bois, T., *Les cerfs-volants et leurs applications militaires*, Paris, 1906.

Bourne, W., *Inventions or Devises*, London, 1578, p. 99.

Brisbane, Sir T., 'Observations made at Port Macquarie, Van Dieman's Land, for the purpose of determining the Decrease of Heat in Ascending in the Atmosphere', *The Edinburgh Journal of Science*, Vol. 6, 1827, pp. 246–9.

Broomfield, G. A., *Pioneer of the Air: the Life and Times of Colonel S. F. Cody*, Aldershot, 1953.

Brown, Rev. G., *Melanesians and Polynesians*, London, 1910, p. 323.

Bruce, E. S., 'Some Forms of Scientific Kites', *Quarterly Journal of the Royal Meteorological Society*, Vol. 35, No. 149, Jan. 1909, pp. 31–5.

Bryant, L. W., *et al.*, *Collected Researches on the Stability of Kites and Towed Gliders*, London, 1950.

Cardano, G., *De rerum varietate libri xvii*, Basel, 1557, p. 440.

Cavallo, T., *A Complete Treatise on Electricity*, London, 1777, pp. 330–8.

★Chadwick, N. K., 'The Kite: a Study in Polynesian Tradition', *JAI*, Vol. 61, 1931, pp. 455–91.

★Chanute, O., *Progress in Flying Machines*, New York, 1894. (Especially pp. 176–97.)

'Chinese Kites', *SA*, Vol. 58, No. 12, March 24, 1888, p. 185.

★Choe Sang-Su, *The Survey of Korean Kites*, Seoul, 1958.

Clayton, H. H., 'A Keel Kite', *The Aeronautical Annual*, 3 vols., Boston, 1895–97, Vol. 3, pp. 151–3.

Codrington, R. H., *The Melanesians*, Oxford, 1891, pp. 318, 336, 342.

Cody, S. F., 'The New Observation Kites Invented by S. F. Cody', *SAS*, Vol. 55, No. 1423, April 11, 1903, p. 22,804.

'The Cody Kites', *SAS*, Vol. 57, No. 1468, Feb. 20, 1904, p. 23,524. (Cody's Channel crossing.)

Colenso, W., 'Reminiscences of the Ancient Maoris', *Transactions and Proceedings of the New Zealand Institute, 1891*, Vol. 24, 1892, pp. 465–6.

Colladon, D., 'Expériences sur les cerfs-volants', *La Nature*, Vol. 15, No. 757, July 16, 1887, pp. 97–9.

Corney, B. G. (trans.), *The Quest and Occupation of Tahiti*, 3 vols., London, 1913, Vol. 1, p. 324.

★Culin, S., *Korean Games*, Philadelphia, 1895, pp. 9–21. (Now reissued as *Games of the Orient*, Rutland, Vt., and Tokyo, 1958.)

— 'Hawaiian Games', *American Anthropologist*, n.s., Vol. 1, No. 2, April 1899, pp. 224–6.

Dansey, C. C., 'Kite for effecting a communication between a stranded ship and the shore', *Transactions of the Society For the Encouragement of Arts*, Vol. 41, 1825, pp. 182–9.

Davis, J. W., 'Some Experiments with Kites', *Aeronautics* (N.Y.), Vol. 1, No. 11, Aug. 1894, pp. 153–6.

★Dewall, H. A., 'Het Vliegerspel te Batavia', *Tijdschrift voor Indische Taal-, Land- en Volkenkunde*, Vol. 50, 1908, pp. 414–33.

Dillaye, F., *Les jeux de la jeunesse*, Paris, 1885, pp. 33–42.

Dines, W. H., 'Scientific Kite Flying', *Nature*, Vol. 68, No. 1755, June 18, 1903, pp. 154–5.

Dines, W. H. and Shaw, W. N., *The Free Atmosphere in the Region of the British Isles*, London, 1909.

The Domestic Encyclopedia or, a Dictionary of Facts and Useful Knowledge, 4 vols., London, 1802, Vol. 3, 'Kite, Electrical', and 'Lightning'.

Doolittle, Rev. J., *Social Life of the Chinese*, 2 vols., London, 1866, Vol. 2, pp. 70–1.

Downer, M., *Kites: How to Make and Fly Them*, New York, 1959. (Ch.)

★Duhem, J., *Histoire des idées aéronautiques avant Montgolfier*, 2 vols., Paris, 1943. (Esp. Vol. 1, pp. 194–202.)

Dundonald, T., *The Autobiography of a Seaman*, 2 vols., London, 1860, Vol. 1, p. 201.

★Eddy, W. A., 'Experiments with Hexagon and Tailless Kites', *Aeronautics* (N.Y.), Vol. 1, No. 11, Aug. 1894, pp. 152–3.

— 'Photographing from Kites', *The Century Illustrated Monthly Magazine*, Vol. 54, No. 1, May 1897, pp. 86–91.

— 'Some Kite Records in the United States', *AJ*, Vol. 3, No. 1, Jan. 1899, pp. 15–16.

★— 'A Record of Some Kite Experiments', *MWR*, Vol. 26, No. 10, Oct. 1898, pp. 450–2.

Edge-Partington, T. W., *An Album of the Weapons, Tools, Ornaments, Articles of Dress &c. of the Natives of the Pacific Islands*, [1st s.] Manchester, 1890, pp. 150, 197; 2nd s., Manchester, 1895, p. 79.

— 'Kite Fishing by the Salt-water Natives of Mala or Malaita Island, British Solomon Islands', *Man*, Vol. 12, 1912, pp. 9–11.

Ellis, W., *Polynesian Researches*, 2 vols., London, 1829, Vol. 1, p. 310.

Emerson, J. S., 'A Kite-Flying Invocation from Hawaii', *American Anthropologist*, n.s., Vol. 23, No. 3, July–Sept., 1921, pp. 386–7.

Espy, J. P., *The Philosophy of Storms*, Boston, 1841.

'Essai de l'appareil Simmons', *l'Aéronaute*, Vol. 9, No. 11, Nov. 1876, pp. 313–4.

'Experiment made at the Kew Observatory on a new Kite-Apparatus for Meteorological Observations, or other purposes', *The London, Edinburgh, and Dublin Philosophical Magazine and Journal of Science*, Vol. 31, No. 207, Sept. 1847, pp. 191–2.

★Feldhaus, F. M., *Die Technik der Vorzeit*, Leipzig & Berlin, 1914, cols. 650–9. (Excellent illustrations of windsock-kites.)

★Fergusson, S. P., 'Exploration of the Air by Means of Kites', *Annals of the Astronomical Observatory of Harvard College*, Vol. 42, Pt. 1, 1896, pp. 41–128.

Fowler, H. W., *Kites*, New York, 1953. (Ch.)

★Franklin, B., *Benjamin Franklin's Autobiographical Writings*, Selected and edited by Carl van Doren, New York, 1945, pp. 3–4.

— *The Papers of Benjamin Franklin*, Ed. L. W. Labaree, Vol. 4, New Haven, 1961, pp. 360–9.

Garber, P. E., *Kites and Kite Flying*, New York, 1931. (Ch.).

— *U.S. Navy Target Kites*, Washington, 1944.

Gardiner, J. S., 'The Natives of Rotuma', *JAI*, Vol. 27, 1897, pp. 487–8.

Gellius, Aulus, *Noctium atticarum libri xx*, Book x, Chapter 12, para. 8.

'General Butler an Inventor', *SA*, Vol. 11, No. 6, Aug. 6, 1864, p. 82.

The Gentleman's Magazine, Vol. 16, 1746, p. 431.

Gerini, G. E., 'Festivals and Fasts (Siamese)', In Hastings' *Encyclopedia of Religion and Ethics*, Vol. 5, p. 888.

★Gibbs-Smith, C. H., *The Aeroplane: an Historical Survey*, London, 1960, pp. 161–3.

★— *Sir George Cayley's Aeronautics 1796–1855*, London, 1962.

★— *The Invention of the Aeroplane*, London, 1966.

★Gill, W. W., *Myths and Songs from the South Pacific*, London, 1876, pp. 122–4.

★— *From Darkness to Light in Polynesia*, London, 1894, pp. 39–44.

'Glossary of Flex Wing Vehicles', *Ryan Reporter*, Vol. 25, No. 2, Summer 1964, pp. 7–9.

Gold, E., *The International Kite and Balloon Ascents*, London, 1913. (Met. reports only.)

Gordon, L., *Peepshow into Paradise: A History of Children's Toys*, London, 1953, pp. 169–70.

Grabowsky, F., 'Spiele und Spielzeuge bei den Dajaken Südost-Borneos', *Globus*, Vol. 73, 1898, p. 376.

Grahame, A., 'Target Kite Imitates Plane's Flight', *Popular Science Monthly*, Vol. 146, No. 5, May 1945, pp. 65–7.

*de Groot, J. J. M., *Les Fêtes annuellement célébrées à Emoui*, Paris, 1886, Pt. 2, pp. 530–7.

*Grosvenor, G. H., 'The Tetrahedral Kites of Dr Alexander Graham Bell', *Popular Science Monthly*, Vol. 64, No. 2, Dec. 1903, pp. 131–51.

— 'Dr Bell's Man-Lifting Kite', *NGM*, Vol. 19, No. 1, Jan. 1908, pp. 35–52.

*Haddon, A. C., *The Study of Man*, London, 1898, pp. 232–54.

*Hargrave, L., 'Cellular Kites', *Engineering*, Vol. 56, Oct. 27, 1893, pp. 523–4.

— 'Flying Machine Motors and Cellular Kites', *JPRSNSW*, Vol. 27, 1893, pp. 75–81.

— 'Experiments on Kites', *Engineering*, Vol. 59, Feb. 15, 1895, p. 221. (See also p. 320.)

— 'Paper on Aeronautical Work', *JPRSNSW*, Vol. 29, 1895, pp. 40–7.

— 'On the Cellular Kite', *JPRSNSW*, Vol. 30, 1896, pp. 144–7.

— 'The Possibility of Soaring in Horizontal Wind', *JPRSNSW*, Vol. 31, 1897, pp. 207–13.

— 'Aeronautics', *JPRSNSW*, Vol. 32, 1898, pp. 55–65.

*— 'Soaring Machines', *JPRSNSW*, Vol. 32, 1898, pp. 209–22.

*— 'Rigid Stable Aeroplanes', *JPRSNSW*, Vol. 43, 1909, pp. 381–7.

Harmand, J., 'Sur le cerf-volant musical du Camboge', *La Nature*, Vol. 9, No. 404, Feb. 26, 1881, pp. 202–3.

Hart, C., *Your Book of Kites*, London, 1964. (Ch.)

Hartwig, G., *The Aerial World*, London, 1886, pp. 29–30.

Hennig, R., 'Beiträge zur Frühgeschichte der Aeronautik', *Beiträge zur Geschichte der Technik und Industrie*, Vol. 8, 1918, pp. 100–16.

Henningsen, P., *P.H.s dragebog for børn fra 8–128 år*, Copenhagen, 1955. (Ch.)

Henry, A. J., 'A Weather Bureau Kite–How It Is Constructed', *SAS*, Vol. 70, No. 1826, Dec. 31, 1910, pp. 428–9.

Henry, T., *Ancient Tahiti*, Honolulu, 1928, p. 279.

Hervey, D. F. A., 'Malay Games', *JAI*, Vol. 33, 1903, pp. 291–2.

Hill, A. H., 'Some Kelantan Games and Entertainments', *Journal of the Malayan Branch of the Royal Asiatic Society*, Vol. 25, Pt. 1, Aug. 1952, pp. 26–8.

Hirn, Y., 'Pappersdraken', In *Festskrift tillegnad Edvard Westermarck*, Helsingfors, 1912, pp. 293–304.

— *Barnlek*, Helsingfors, 1916, pp. 49–69.

Hiroa, Te Rangi (Peter H. Buck), *Arts and Crafts of the Cook Islands*, Honolulu, 1944, pp. 257–9.

*Hodgson, J. E., *The History of Aeronautics in Great Britain*, Oxford, 1924. (Esp. pp. 368–72.)

Holmes, J. H., 'Introductory Notes on the Toys and Games of Elema, Papuan Gulf', *JAI*, Vol. 38, 1908, p. 282.

Hooke, R., Royal Society Library, classified papers, Vol. 20, Item 54r.

— *The Diary of Robert Hooke*, ed. H. W. Robinson and W. Adams, London, 1935, p. 146.

Hooper, W., *Rational Recreations*, 4 vols., London, 1774, Vol. 3, pp. 82–90. ('The electrical kite', mostly from de Romas.)

*Houard, G., *Les Ascensions en cerfs-volants*, Paris, 1911.

Hubbard, T. O'B., 'British Aeronautics in the 17th Century', *Aeronautics*, London, Vol. 4, Oct. 1911, p. 186.

Hunt, L. L., *25 Kites that Fly*, Milwaukee, 1929. (Ch.)

Hurgronje, C. S., *The Achehnese*, 2 vols., Leyden and London, 1906, Vol. 2, p. 191.

Instructions for Making Aerological Observations, Washington, 1930, pp. 2–67. (Technical details of kite-meteorology in its later stages.)

Jackson, F. N., *Toys of Other Days*, London, 1908, pp. 250–4.

Jobert, C., 'Expériences télégraphiques exécutées avec des cerfs-volants', *l'Aéronaute*, Vol. 11, No. 4, April 1878.

— 'Un cerf-volant porte-amarre à cone', *l'Aéronaute*, Vol. 20, No. 3, March 1887, pp. 43–6.

Kettelkamp, L., *Kites*, London, 1961. (Ch.)

Kijang Puteh, 'Malay Kites', *Straits Times Annual*, 1962, pp. 8–11.

*Kircher, A., *Ars magna lucis et umbrae*, Rome, 1646, Pt. 2, pp. 826–7.

Kite Drill. [London, 1910.] (Publication of the London Balloon Company, Royal Engineers. Only 100 copies printed.)

Kites and Kite Making, Washington, 1930. (U.S. Weather Bureau publication, with full technical details.)

*Kyeser, K., *Bellifortis* [*ca.* 1405], Niedersächsische Staats- und Universitätsbibliothek, Göttingen, Codex 63, ff. 104v., 105r.

*— *Bellifortis* [*ca.* 1410], Badische Landesbibliothek, Karlsruhe, Codex Durlach 11, f. 119r.

LaBerge, A. J., *Boats, Airplanes, and Kites*, Peoria, 1935. (Ch.)

*Lamson, C. H., 'Work on the Great Diamond', *The Aeronautical Annual*, 3 vols., Boston, 1895–97, Vol. 2, pp. 133–7.

*'Lamson's Kite–Trial of a Kite Carrying one Hundred and Fifty Pounds', *SA*, Vol. 75, No. 9, Aug. 1896, p. 191.

'Lamson's New Kite', *AJ*, Vol. 3, No. 1, Jan. 1899, pp. 16–17.

Lana, F. de, *Prodromo, overo saggio di alcune inventioni*, Brescia, 1670, pp. 50–51.

Landreau ['Communication au sujet de l'appareil Simmons'], *l'Aéronaute*, Vol. 9, No. 4, April 1876, pp. 116–7.

*Laufer, B., *The Prehistory of Aviation*, Chicago, 1928.

LeBailly, C., *Les Cerfs-volants: comment les construire, comment les utiliser*, Paris, n.d. (Ch.)

*Lecornu, J., *Les Cerfs-volants*, Paris, 1902. (2nd edn., 1910.)

Lee, A. G., *The Flying Cathedral*, London, 1965. (Biography of Cody.)

Leloup, J., 'Les cerfs-volants militaires au XIme siècle', *l'Aéronaute*, Vol. 39, No. 8, Aug. 1906, pp. 142–4.

Lestoire de Merlin, Ed. H. O. Sommer, Washington, 1908.

*'Life Saving Devices', *SAS*, Vol. 34, 1892, pp. 13,803–4, 13,917, 13,965.

La Loubère, S. de, *Historical Relation of the Kingdom of Siam*, London, 1693, p. 49.

Luang Sithisayamkarn, *Some Useful Information on the Buddhist Religion*, Bangkok, 1963, pp. 81–98.

McAdie, A., 'Franklin's Kite Experiment with Modern Apparatus', *Popular Science Monthly*, Vol. 51, Oct. 1897, pp. 739–47.

McDowell, C., Jr., 'It's Limp but it Flies', *Richmond Times-Dispatch Magazine*, Dec. 18, 1949. (Rogallo kites.)

*Maillot [Notes on large kite], *l'Aéronaute*, Vol. 19, No. 7, July 1886, pp. 134–8.

'Man Carrying Kites', *SA*, Vol. 132, Feb. 1925, p. 124.

'Man-Lifting Kites', *AJ*, Vol. 9, No. 1, Jan. 1905, pp. 16–18.

Marconi, D., *My Father, Marconi*, London, 1962, pp. 100 ff.

Marsh, W. L., *Aeronautical Prints & Drawings*, London, 1924, Plate 2.

*Marvin, C. F., *Kite Experiments at the Weather Bureau*, Washington, 1897.

*— *The Mechanics and Equilibrium of Kites*, Washington, 1897.

Means, J., 'The Kite Considered as an Instrument of Value', *The Aeronautical Annual*, 3 vols., Boston, 1895–97, Vol. 2, pp. 111–118.

Means, J. H., *James Means and the Problem of Manflight*, Washington, 1964.

*Milemete, W. de, *De nobilitatibus, sapientiis, et prudentiis regum*, Ed. M. R. James, London, 1913, pp. 154–5.

Miller, C. M., *The Construction and Flying of Kites*, Peoria, 1909.

— *Kite Craft*, Worcester, Mass., 1910.

— *Kitecraft and Kite Tournaments*, Peoria, 1914.

Millet, J. B., 'The Malay Kite', *The Aeronautical Annual*, 3 vols., Boston, 1895–97, Vol. 2, pp. 119–26.

— 'Some Experiences with Hargrave Kites', *The Aeronautical Annual*, 3 vols., Boston, 1895–97, Vol. 2, pp. 127–32.

— 'Scientific Kite Flying', *The Century Illustrated Monthly Magazine*, Vol. 54, No. 1, May 1897, pp. 66–77.

Miyawaki, T., *Tako: Japanese Kite Book*, Tokyo and Rutland, Vt., 1962. (Ch.)

Moedebeck, H. W. L., *Taschenbuch zum praktischen Gebrauch für Flugtechniker und Luftschiffer*, 3rd edn., Berlin, 1911, pp. 149–70.

Moffett, C., 'Scientific Kite Flying', *McClure's Magazine*, Vol. 6, No. 4, March 1896, pp. 379–92. (Mostly about Eddy.)

Moore, W. R., 'Scintillating Siam', *NGM*, Vol. 91, No. 2, Feb. 1947, pp. 194, 197.

*Morse, E. S., *Japan Day by Day*, Tokyo, 1936, Pt. 2, pp. 87, 142, 178–9, 388–91, 399.

Morwood, J., *Sailing Aerodynamics*, Southampton, 1962, pp. 86–8.

Moule, A. C., 'A List of the Musical and other Sound-Producing Instruments of the Chinese', *Journal of the Royal Asiatic Society, North China Branch*, Vol. 39, 1908, p. 105.

*Müller, W., *Der Papierdrachen in Japan*, Stuttgart, 1914.

*Musschenbroek, P. van, *Introductio ad philosophiam naturalem*, Leyden, 1762, Vol. 1, pp. 177, 295–6.

Myers, C. E., 'The Texas Dynamite Kites and Application of Kites to Aerial Photography–Kite Flying Without Tail or String–Self-Flying Kites', *SAS*, Vol. 33, No. 835, Jan. 2, 1892, pp. 13,348–9.

*Nares, Sir G., *Seamanship*, Portsmouth, 1886, pp. 276–80.

Neal, H. E., *The Story of the Kite*, New York, 1954. (Ch.)

*Needham, J., *Science and Civilisation in China*, Vol. 4, Pt. 2, Cambridge, 1965, pp. 568–602. (The most authoritative summary of the history of kites in China.)

Nissen, W., and Horstenke, B., *Lustige Windvögel: ein Buch von Drachenbau und Drachensport*, Ravensburg, 1953. (Ch.)

Onslow [Note on kiting partridge], *Notes and Queries*, Vol. 182, No. 11, March 14, 1942, p. 152. (See also Vol. 182, No. 16, April 18, 1942, p. 223.)

*Parkin, J. H., *Bell and Baldwin*, Toronto, 1964.

*Plischke, H., *Der Fischdrachen*, Leipzig, 1922.

*— 'Alter und Herkunft des Europäischen Flächendrachens', *Nachrichten von der Gesellschaft der Wissenschaften zu Göttingen*, Phil.-Hist. Kl., N.F., Fachgr. 2, Vol. 2, No. 1, 1936, pp. 1–18. (The first thorough, though somewhat inaccurate, treatment of the subject.)

*Pocock, G., *The Aeropleustic Art, or Navigation in the Air by the Use of Kites, or Buoyant Sails*, London, 1827 (2nd edn., 1851).

Polo, M., *The Description of the World*, Ed. A. C. Moule and P. Pelliot, 2 vols., London, 1938, Vol. I, pp. 356–7.

*Porta, G. B. della, *Magiae naturalis . . . libri iiii*, Naples, 1558, pp. 69–70. (English trans. by T. Young and S. Speed: *Natural Magick*, London, 1658.)

Poujoula, R., *Le cerf-volant de sauvetage*, Paris, 1913.

Priestley, J., *History and Present State of Electricity*, London, 1767, pp. 171–2.

Pritchard, J. L., *Sir George Cayley, the Inventor of the Aeroplane*, London, 1961.

Rausch, H. A., 'Die Spiele der Jugend aus Fischarts Gargantua', *Jahrbuch für Geschichte, Sprache und Literatur Elsass-Lothringens*, Vol. 24, 1908, pp. 53 ff.

Reed, A. W., *Games the Maoris Played*, Wellington, 1958, pp. 4–5. (Ch.)

Reveley, H. W., 'The Shipwreck Kite', *Journal of the Society of Arts*, Vol. 9, No. 440, April 26, 1861, pp. 433–4. (Eighteen-ft. Dansey kite, equipped with two guy-lines. Once used to draw a carriage, *ca.* 1824.)

Ridgway, H., *Kite Making and Flying*, London, 1962. (Ch.)

*Rogallo, F. M., 'First Flexible Kite', *Ford Times*, March 1951, pp. 25–9.

*— 'Parawings for Astronautics', NASA publication, 1963. (Contains a bibliography of publications on flex-wings.)

*Romain, C., *Les cerfs-volants observatoires*, Paris, 1913.

*de Romas, J., *Mémoire, sur les moyens de se garantir de la foudre dans les maisons*, Bordeaux, 1776.

*— *Oeuvres inédites*, Ed. J. Bergonié, Bordeaux, 1911.

Rotch, A. L., 'On Obtaining Meteorological Records in the Upper Air by Means of Kites and Balloons', *Proceedings of the American Academy of Arts and Sciences*, Vol. 32, No. 13, May 1897.

*— 'The Exploration of the Free Air by Means of Kites at Blue Hill Observatory, Massachusetts', *Annual Report of the Smithsonian Institution, 1897*, Washington, 1898, pp. 317–24.

— 'Progress in the Exploration of the Air with Kites at the Blue Hill Observatory, Massachusetts', *MWR*, Vol. 26, No. 8, Aug. 1898, pp. 355–6.

— *Sounding the Ocean of Air*, London, 1900, pp. 117–44.

*— 'The Use of Kites to Obtain Meteorological Observations', *Annual Report of the Smithsonian Institution, 1900*, Washington, 1901, pp. 223–31.

— 'The Exploration of the Atmosphere at Sea by Means of Kites', *Annual Report of the Smithsonian Institution, 1901*, Washington, 1902, pp. 245–9.

— 'Kites and Wireless Telegraphy', *Nature*, Vol. 65, No. 1679, Jan. 2, 1902, p. 198. (Rotch says he sent telegraphic messages over kite-wires before Marconi, in the summer of 1899.)

*Roughley, T. C., *The Aeronautical Work of Lawrence Hargrave*, Sydney, 1937. (Rev. edn., 1939.)

**Rüst- und Feuerwerksbuch* [ca. 1490], Stadt- und Universitätsbibliothek Frankfurt am Main, f. 104r.

*Saconney, J. T., *Cerfs-volants militaires*, Paris, 1909.

Salmon, S. H. R., 'Across-Channel Communication by Kite', *AJ*, Vol. 10, No. 3, July 1906, pp. 44–5.

Schmidlap, J., *Künstliche und rechtschaffene Feuerwerck zum schimpff*, Nürnberg, 1608, p. 4. (Written 1560.)

Schneider, K., 'Die Hochaufstiege am Observatorium Lindenberg', *Die Arbeiten des Preussischen Aeronautischen Observatoriums bei Lindenberg*, Vol. 14, 1922, pp. 150–7.

*Schweisguth, P., 'Note sur les jeux de cerf-volants en Thailande', *Journal of the Siam Society*, Vol. 34. (The most thorough account of Thai kite-flying.)

*Schwenter, D., *Deliciae physico-mathematicae*, Nürnberg, 1636, Pt. 12, pp. 472–5.

Seemann, B., *Viti*, Cambridge, 1862, p. 45.

de Serière, V., 'Javasche volksspelen en vermaken', *Tijdschrift voor Nederlandsch Indië*, n.s., Vol. 2, 1873, Pt. 1, pp. 84–8.

Shaw, W. H., 'Aeronautical work of Lawrence Hargrave', *Shell Aviation News*, Vol. 289, 1962, pp. 2–7.

★— 'Lawrence Hargrave-an Appreciation', *JPRSNSW*, Vol. 96, Pts. 2–6, 1963, pp. 17–30.

— 'Lawrence Hargrave, Aviation Pioneer', *Aircraft*, Jan. 1964.

Shaw, W. N., *Manual of Meteorology*, 4 vols., Cambridge, 1926–36. (Especially Vol. 1, 'Meteorology in History'.)

Singh, D. J., *Classic Cooking from India*, London, 1958. (Pp. 142–4 contain an excellent account of Indian kite-flying.)

Skeat, W. W., *Malay Magic*, London, 1900, pp. 484–5.

Strutt, J., *The Sports and Pastimes of the People of England*, London, 1801.

Swaim, J., 'Electro-Meteorological Observations', *The American Journal of Science and Arts*, 1st s., Vol. 32, No. 2, July 1837, pp. 304–7.

Swan, J., *Speculum Mundi or a Glasse representing the Face of the World*, Cambridge, 1635, p. 93.

Tachard, *Second voyage du père Tachard*, Paris, 1689, pp. 256–7.

Taylor, J. W. R., *A Picture History of Flight*, London, 1959, p. 12. (Kites as invasion weapons in the Napoleonic Wars.)

Taylor, R., *Te Ika a Maui; or, New Zealand and its Inhabitants*, London, 1870, p. 346.

Teisserenc de Bort, L., 'Sur les ascensions dans l'atmosphère d'enrégistreurs météoro-logiques portés par des cerfs-volants', *Comptes rendues des séances de l'Académie des Sciences*, Vol. 129, 1899, pp. 131–2.

Thien Chia, *Fang Fêng Chêng*, 1957.

Thomson, B., *The Fijians: A Study of the Decay of Custom*, London, 1908, pp. 93–4.

★Tissandier, G., 'Les cerfs-volants japonais', *La Nature*, Vol. 14, No. 699, Oct. 25, 1886, pp. 332–4.

★— 'Cerfs-volants chinois', *La Nature*, Vol. 16, No. 759, Dec. 17, 1887, pp. 44–6.

'Traction by Kites', *The Engineer*, Vol. 90, Aug. 24, 1900, p. 193.

Tregear, E., 'The Maoris of New Zealand', *JAI*, Vol. 19, 1890, p. 115.

— (trans.) 'The Maori Kite of Aute Bark', *Journal of the Polynesian Society*, Vol. 10, 1901, pp. 192–3. (See also pp. 169, 204–5.)

Tylor, E. B., 'The History of Games', *Fortnightly Review*, n.s., Vol. 25, 1879, pp. 35–6.

— 'Remarks on the Geographical Distribution of Games', *JAI*, Vol. 9, 1880, pp. 25–6.

'Une Nouvelle espèce de cerf-volant', *Le Magasin Pittoresque*, Vol. 40, 1873, p. 280.

Varney, G. J., 'Kite-Flying in 1897', *Popular Science Monthly*, Vol. 53, No. 1, May 1898, pp. 48–63.

Voisin, G., *Men, Women and 10,000 Kites*, London, 1963. (Accounts of Voisin develop-ments.)

von Bassermann-Jordan, E., *Alte Uhren und ihre Meister*, Leipzig, 1926, pp. 64–6.

★Wales, H. G. Q., *Siamese State Ceremonies*, London, 1931, pp. 221–2.

Walker, F., *Practical Kites and Aeroplanes*, London, 1903. (Rev. edn., 1909.)

*Walsh, Rev. P., 'The Manuaute, or Maori Kite', *Transactions and Proceedings of the New Zealand Institute, 1912*, Vol. 45, pp. 375–84.

Weber, M., H.M. *'Siboga' Expedition, 1899–1900*, Leiden, 1902, pp. 60–1.

Wecker, J., *De secretis libri xvii*, Basel, 1582, pp. 690–2, 936–8.

*Wenham, F. H., 'On Aërial Locomotion', *First Annual Report of the Aëronautical Society of Great Britain*, London, 1866. (Man-lifting kites, pp. 30–3.)

Wen[t]z, E., 'Note sur l'enlèvement d'un cerf-volant par un temps calme au moyen d'une automobile', *l'Aéronaute*, Vol. 32, No. 4, April 1899, pp. 87–90.

— 'La Photographie aérienne par cerfs-volants', *l'Aérophile*, Vol. 10, No. 12, Dec. 1902, pp. 304–6.

*Westervelt, W. D., *Legends of Ma-ui, a Demi God*, Honolulu, 1910, pp. 87, 114–18, 128.

*Whitnah, D. R., *A History of the United States Weather Bureau*, Urbana, 1961.

Wilkinson, R. J., *Life and Customs in Malaya*, Kuala Lumpur, 1910, Pt. 3, pp. 19–21.

Williams, C. A. S., *Encyclopedia of Chinese Symbolism and Art Motives*, New York, 1960, pp. 11–14.

Wilson, P., 'Biographical Account of Alexander Wilson', *Transactions of the Royal Society of Edinburgh*, Vol. 10, 1826, pp. 284–7.

Wise, H. D., 'Experiments with Kites', *The Century Illustrated Monthly Magazine*, Vol. 54, No. 1, May 1897, pp. 78–86.

*— 'Flying in the Beginning', *SA*, Vol. 147, Sept. 1932, pp. 140–1, 186–7; Oct., pp. 212–3, 251.

Woglom, G. T., *Parakites*, New York, 1896.

Wright, G. N., *China*, 4 vols., London, 1843, Vol. 4, pp. 6–7: 'Kite-flying at Hae-Kwan'.

Wright, W. and O., *The Papers of Wilbur and Orville Wright*, Ed. M. W. McFarland, 2 vols., New York, 1953.

Yolen, W., *The Young Sportsman's Guide to Kite Flying*, New York, 1963. (Ch.)

Young, T., *A Course of Lectures on Natural Philosophy*, 2 vols., London, 1807, Vol. I, p. 324.

Zimmerman[n], C., 'A New Form of Aeroplane', *AJ*, Vol. 2, No. 3, July 1898, pp. 64–5.

GENERAL REFERENCES

The following are a few of the more important publications containing further articles and notes of interest:

l'Aéronaute (Paris)

The Aeronatical Journal (London)

Aeronautics (London)

Aeronautics (New York)

l'Aérophile (Paris)

le Cerf-volant; la Revue du cerf-volant (Paris. As far as I know, these journals, which ran for a few years from 1909, are the only ones ever to have been devoted primarily to kites as objects of serious technological interest.)

Illustrierte Aëronautische Mitteilungen (Strassburg)

Kites Lines (Baltimore, Maryland. Quarterly journal of the world-wide kite community. Sucessor to *Kite Tales* since 1977.)

Kite Tales (Silver City, New Mexico. Quarterly Publication of the American Kite-fliers Association from 1964 to 1976.)

Monthly Weather Review (Washington. Between about 1895 and 1915 this journal published many articles on the practical applications of the kite.)

Scientific American; Scientific American Supplement (New York)

Zeitschrift für Luftschiffahrt (Berlin)

CHECK-LIST OF ADDITIONAL MATERIAL

The Adventures of a Kite. London, n.d. (*ca.* 1850.)

Bacon, P. *The Kite. An Heroi-Comical Poem. In Three Canto's.* Oxford, 1722.

Bélèze, G. *Jeux des adolescents.* Paris, 1856, pp. 146-52.

The Book of Games; or a history of the juvenile sports practised at the Kingston Academy. London, 1805, pp. 47-57.

Edgeworth, M. *Harry and Lucy Concluded.* 4 vols. London, 1825, vol. 4, pp. 288-96.

Euler, L. 'Des cerfs-volans.' *Histoire de l'Académie Royale des Sciences et Belles Lettres, année MDCCLVI.* Berlin, 1758, pp. 322-64 and Figs. I and II, following p. 386.

Graffigny, H. de. *Les cerfs-volants.* Paris, 1910.

Hart, Clive. *The Dream of Flight: Aeronautics from Classical Times to the Renaissance.* London, 1972.

— 'Another Flying Dragon.' *AJ*, vol. 76, September 1972, p. 551.

Les jeux de la jeunesse: ou nouvelle méthode à instruire les enfans. Newmarket, 1814, pp. 34-6.

Les jeux des jeunes garçons. 4th edn. Paris, n.d. (early 19th century.) Part 2, pp.13-21.

'The Kite, A Fable; or, Pride Must Have a Fall.' *The Child's Reward Book, containing several narratives, peculiarly interesting to young persons.* Part I. London, n.d. (*ca.* 1820.)

Lecornu, J. *De l'emploi des trains de cerfs-volants montés.* Paris, 1917.

— *Sous-marins et cerfs-volants.* Paris, 1917.

A Little Pretty Pocket-Book Intended for the Instruction and Amusement of Little Master Tommy, and Pretty Miss Polly . . . 10th edn. London, 1760, B3ᵛ.

'On the flying of a paper kite.' *A Choice Selection of Hymns and Moral Songs.* Newcastle, 1781, pp. 110-11.

Pinon, R. 'Le jeu du cerf-volant en Wallonie.' *Mélanges de linguistique romane et de philologie médiévale offerts à M. Maurice Delbouille.* 2 vols. Gembloux, 1964, vol. I, pp. 489-516.

Quentin, H. *La photographie par cerfs-volants.* Paris, n.d. (*ca.* 1910.)

Shaw, W. Hudson, and Ruhen, Olaf. *Lawrence Hargrave: Explorer, Inventor & Aviation Experimenter.* Stanmore, NSW, 1977.

Stories of Instruction and Delight. London, 1802. (Two pictures and a brief story; n.p.)

Ter Gouw, J. *De Volksvermaken.* Haarlem, 1871, pp. 295, 319-20.

ANNOTATED KITE BIBLIOGRAPHY

For an excellent annotated check-list of mainly recent material, see: *Annotated Kite Bibliography.* Baltimore MD, 1979. (Published by *Kite Lines.*)

Index

Index

Index